THE WANDERER

CAROLE J. GARRISON

THE WANDERER

FLORIDA | NEW YORK
www.2leafpress.org

P.O. Box 4378
Grand Central Station
New York, New York 10163-4378
editor@2leafpress.org
www.2leafpress.org

2LEAF PRESS INC. is a
nonprofit 501(c)(3) organization that promotes
multicultural literature and literacy.
www.2lpinc.org

Copy editing: Ben Lafferty

Book design and layout: Gabrielle David

Library of Congress Control Number: 2020932738

ISBN-13: 978-1-7346181-1-2 (Paperback)
ISBN-13: 978-1-7346181-4-3 (eBook)

10　9　8　7　6　5　4　3　2　1

Published in the United States of America

2Leaf Press trade distribution is handled by University of Chicago Press / Chicago Distribution Center (www.press.uchicago.edu) 773.702.7010. Titles are also available for corporate, premium, and special sales. Please direct inquiries to the UCP Sales Department, 773.702.7248.

To my fellow wanderers, hosts, and guides; to the QQ's and other strangers who are now friends; and to Gabrielle who said "write it down."

CONTENTS

INTRODUCTION

Decades have past since I sat in my parked car outside the tall chain linked fence that lined the runway at Miami international airport listening to the pilots talk to the control tower. I held a peanut butter and jelly sandwich in one hand while holding a bottle of milk for the baby in the other. While I nibbled and my toddler drank, I would fantasize being on one of those airplanes going somewhere, going anywhere.

By the 1980s, I was traveling to attend conferences as an academic, or to consult with the Department of Defense on women in the military. I journeyed around the world with my mother visiting my husband's foreign graduate students or their families. But in 1992 when I volunteered with the United Nations to help super-vise elections in Cambodia following the Paris Peace Accords that ended years of civil war and the Khmer Rouge's killing spree of close to three million Cambodians, it changed my life. My international friends list grew exponentially and provided me with travel destinations pretty much all over the world.

In addition, international students came in increasing numbers to the graduate program at Eastern Kentucky University in the early years of the twenty-first century while I was chair of the Criminal Justice Department.

The students came mainly from Turkey and Russia, and I became a surrogate parent, mentor, and friend to most of them. After they returned home, I added them to my travel itinerary whenever a visit was possible. Few of my former students had either the resources or the desire to visit me in Ohio, Kentucky, or West Virginia—states I called home, where there were few extraordinary attractions to offer. If they did come to the U.S., they visited California (Disneyland was a big draw) or Washington, D. C. So I was welcomed to their homes with outrageous hospitality; the price of my visit was an authentic, earnest interest in their lives.

In the fall of 2017 I had a serious and sustained bout of arthritis. My mortality hung in the air around me, settled in the sheets I slept in, invaded my dreams and my waking consciousness. I needed to feel alive. Traveling made me feel alive. The itinerary for this journey was the culmination of life experiences, people and places I had met along the way, philosophies and interests I had cultivated in my seventy plus years. No deeper than that, and no less consequential, because my life had been rich in experiences and friendships. I wanted to revisit some of those and at the same time, I was hungry to discover something new, things you might add to a bucket list. This is a travel journal of that trip around the world in 2018, revisiting friends as well as traveling to the places on my bucket list. ∎

CHAPTER PHOTO CREDIT: Airport terminal in Chengdu, China. *The Carole J. Garrison Family Archive.*

Airport terminal in Reykjavik, Iceland. *The Carole J. Garrison Family Archive.*

1 When Your Shock Absorbers Fail

I chose to make a spontaneous trip to Geneva to surprise an old friend upon her retirement from the International Red Cross, and then take a quick hop over to Podgorica in Montenegro to visit another longtime friend, who was beginning a six-month electoral mission with the European Centre for Electoral Support. What could be more adventurous, more exciting? It was both of those things, until it wasn't.

The pain started deep in my inner thigh, waking me from a sound sleep three nights before my scheduled departure from West Virginia. By morning, it had turned into an ache that moved down toward my knee and a slight burning sensation up near my groin. *Damn arthritis,* I thought. For several weeks before the advent of the pain, I had felt a bit off— flat and mildly depressed, which I attributed to the onslaught of relentless crazy coming from the Trump

White House. This trip was just the boost I needed to pull myself out of that malaise.

I left home on a Wednesday evening. I spent the day Thursday in bed, sleeping off jet lag. Friday, my one sunny Swiss day, I roamed around the seaside village of Rolle, got sticker shock from a sixty-dollar lunch of perch and fries, and then, feeling a bit tired,

Relaxing with a cup of tea. *The Carole J. Garrison Family Archive.*

caught a phenomenal Swiss train (got to love Swiss infrastructure and chocolate) to Lausanne, where I would hide out until the retirement party on Saturday evening in Geneva.

I felt good on Saturday; my knee ached, but the discomfort was manageable. I dressed in my new leatherette skinny jeggings, black leather boots, and a *très chic* designer blouse. I helped with the floral arrangements, tried out my minimalist French on the other guests, and waited to surprise Kathleen. It was a triumph! But by ten o'clock that night, my thigh burned and my knee ached again. The boots were replaced by sneakers, and my bra was unsnapped and thrown into my bag.

In the middle of the night I woke to use the necessary room, only to find that my entire thigh was covered in a mean red rash. *Frig! Frig! Frig!* Not arthritis, but shingles.

Doctors, meds, bed rest—no, not bed rest, but rather a plane ride to Podgorica to see Beatrice. Finally, after a twelve-hour journey home to West Virginia, I came down with muscular tendonitis in my right shoulder, and the index finger on my right hand became swollen. Coincidence? I don't think so.

According to everything I'd researched on the web, any and all of my recent maladies were most likely stress-related. Apparently, at seventy-five, my shock absorbers had failed. I could no longer roll with the punches thrown by our current government on an hourly basis. I couldn't substitute good thoughts for worries about World War III, or daily needless deaths from gun violence, or women coming forward by the hundreds—the tip of the iceberg—to report sexual abuse and harassment by men they were supposed to trust. Nor could I set aside my concerns about the opioid epidemic, the plight of refugees, the betrayal of

Dreamers, or just the daily insanity of the president's banal tweets that turned the concept of border security into a concrete wall that shut down the government.

When I took my car in to have a bulge in the right front tire fixed, I couldn't help but wonder if the mechanics could repair my own shock absorbers too. ■

CHAPTER PHOTO CREDIT: Me and Beatrice. *The Carole J. Garrison Family Archive.*

2 Finding the Cure

Just as I didn't like looking in the mirror and seeing my mother's eighty-year-old face when I was only fifty, I didn't like thinking about being debilitated at seventy-five; my mom had only been afflicted when she reached her nineties. At fifty I found a good plastic surgeon, had my chin tightened, nose bobbed, and eyebrows lifted.

Curing my latest maladies would not be so simple. I found an arthritis specialist, upped my exercise, reduced my alcohol consumption as well as less salt and sugar, and turned off the nightly news. However, my most radical response was to plan a three-month journey around the world. Like earlier times, I was going to use travel to escape. I had twice used the geographical plan to escape a marriage gone stale, and a couple of times for career re-dos. Why couldn't I do it again, only this time to escape my impending mortality?

DENMARK

FRANCE
- Normandy
- Palaiseau

RUSSIA
- Moscow

TURKEY

MONGOLIA

CHINA
- Xining
- Chengdu

NEPAL BHUTAN

LAOS

CAMBODIA

FUJI
- Nadi

The planning was in a very preliminary phase in December of 2017. I wasn't sure that I was physically up to the trip, so I held off making a final decision, which of course would mean writing a big check to the airline agents who were organizing my 27,000-mile trip to eleven countries. The first several stops would be to visit friends as I traveled east across Europe. Much of the second half was to the Tibetan Buddhist heartland. It was there, I think, I hoped to find the spiritual healing I couldn't find in my own Jewish tradition. Asia, its arts, people and history had always held a place of aesthetic and spiritual magic for me. Finally afraid I would need to recuperate from my journey, I planned an extended stay in Cambodia, which, since my work there in the 1990s, had long been a second home.

Most of the rest were to places unseen, and on my bucket list. I would give the plan a thumbs up or a thumbs down in March, allowing four months to sufficiently rehabilitate myself to make the journey. If you don't think it is possible to experience osteoarthritis, psoriatic arthritis, rheumatoid arthritis, conchritis, and octivitis simultaneously, or occurring as a form of serial torture, let me assure you—it is. I had them all.

In January I worried that the trip would not happen. My university was in a budget crunch and, for reasons that defy logic, it decided to abandon all adjunct professors and part-timers. I depended on teaching my online ethics course in Criminal Justice for an antidote to depression, but now it appeared that the course would be taken from me. Woe to those around me when my days are not filled with things to do or think about. One day I tried to volunteer at the Veterans Administration (VA) to counsel returning veterans on college options. Thanks, but no thanks; the government doesn't accept volunteers. Frustrated, I walked across the broad avenue from the VA offices to Huntington's city hall. It was January 27, the last day to file as a candidate in the upcoming school board election. I put my 25 dollars on the counter and filed. If I wasn't going to teach and couldn't travel, why not run for office? I didn't plan to spend any money on a campaign. Instead, I imagined that meeting people and espousing my views on education would be a great diversion from my pain. Winning was not part of my fantasy.

My school board swearing in. *The Carole J. Garrison Family Archive.*

By March the worst of my symptoms had all but vanished. I wrote the check! I sealed the deal and would leave at the end of July for Denmark, my first stop. However, in April, returning from the traumatic funeral of a former neighbor's son, a very young leukemia victim, I had a major setback—arthritis had attacked my head and neck. I was wretched. In May, still suffering from the renewed onset of arthritis, I received the unsettling news that I had won a seat on the school board and my duties would begin only weeks before I embarked to travel the world. My plans were in shambles.

The school board agreed to let me Skype in for board meetings. A small iPad would keep me connected across multiple time zones. Technology had solved one problem. Packing was another challenge. I wore the heavy hiking boots that I would need for Bhutan and Mongolia, and packed a pair of sneakers and a pair of sandals. My luggage consisted of one medium suitcase containing my clothes and emergency medicine, one backpack with a secret panel for a few thousand dollars in foreign currencies, and one hot pink carry-on bag stuffed full of assorted presents for friends I would stay with along the way—including three dozen miniature squishies, because you never know when you will meet a child who needs a bit of Kawaii "cute." ∎

CHAPTER PHOTO CREDIT: A map of my travels, from Denmark to Fiji.

3 Denmark

"If that mad man wins the presidency, I'm moving to Europe," my niece Marjorie told me over a plate of dim sum in Boston's Chinatown. Very pregnant and trying to manage her rambunctious two-year-old, she showed no sign of hyperbole. I, too, had given thought to leaving the U.S. if Trump were to win, but I still couldn't wrap my mind around his victory being more than a dystopian fantasy. I had, however, underwritten the cost of new passports for my children and grandchildren and had given some thought to Canada—after all, I had family there from my father's side. *Damn, Canada was cold in the winter.* I hoped it wouldn't come to that!

But it did. Trump won; and my niece, seven months pregnant, packed up her home and moved with her husband to Denmark. I stayed in the States, groaning under the weight of my political angst, but doing little about it. I decided that the first stop on my journey around the world would be a visit with Marjorie, who had become a heroine to me.

My plane arrived late to Iceland's Reykjavik airport. I ran past the counter selling fresh smoked salmon, which I had been craving for weeks, and hurried on to my gate. To my delight, the plane to Copenhagen was delayed (thanks be to the travel g-ds), and I went back to buy a fresh bagel and salmon sandwich . . . only to find the gate closed upon my return. The counter agent told me that, if I ran, I could catch another flight to Denmark at a different gate. Once at the new gate, I was sent back to the original gate and, already out of breath, I began running in the reverse direction, hearing "Passenger Garrison, please return to gate 51D." I waved to the agents at the help desk as I ran by. The delayed flight was not a good omen from the travel g-ds, after all.

Now here I must interject a non-sequitur into the story, because there is an important reason that I was able to make the flight. European, and in fact most airports outside the U.S., have two crucial amenities: no charge for carts, and an excess of small complimentary handcarts for carry-on luggage once you pass through security. If I had had to lug my carry-on, bulging with squishies and gifts for friends, without the aid of a push cart, while racing up and down through three terminals in Reykjavik, I would have gone to the hospital, not to Denmark.

Upon arrival in Denmark, I took the commuter train to Copenhagen's central railway station to meet Marjorie. No Marjorie—of course not—the travel g-ds were still not on my side. Instead of her, I found a text message on my phone informing me that Beatrix, age ten months, was in a foul mood, so I should take the next train to an unpronounceable southern provincial town named Næstved, in the unpronounceable region of Sjaelland, on the equally unpronounceable island of the same name. The information people at the train station had never heard of the place I asked about, not with my pronunciation. The ticket machine, once I had worked out where I was going, would not take my credit card without a PIN, which I didn't have. An hour passed before I realized that I could change dollars for Danish krone at the currency exchange—hidden behind a large kiosk—and just buy a ticket at the window. I was spent!

This little corner of Denmark that I visited boasted few attractions. There was however, the Ronnebaek Church—an ageless, beautiful little village church, whitewashed with simple lines. Similar churches dotting the countryside and tucked into villages had caught my interest while on the train trip from Copenhagen to Næstved. I imagined them to be markers of generations, centers of communities, and vigils of time. Næstved's church stood in bright contrast to the big, heavy red brick buildings that filled most of the city center. Marjorie and I satisfied ourselves with long walks through neighboring picturesque town squares, dining on cheap old-man sandwiches bought from carts with a filling combo of crispy pork and a crisp rind, called *Flæskesteg*, and playing with my great niece and nephew.

My android phone burned out—wrong adapter—leaving me with only an iPad and no cellular service.

Our four days together went by quickly, and I prepared to return to Copenhagen and my upcoming flight to Paris. Marjorie—convinced I was an intrepid traveler, with her son Walter's hand firmly gripped in her own—waved goodbye to me at the train station. I boarded with my suitcase, backpack, and too-heavy carry-on. My arthritis was acting up, pain in my wrists and neck making travel difficult at best.

◻ ◉ ◻

Denmark is full of blond, blue-eyed children and adults with fair skin and a striking resemblance to the cast of the TV show, *Vikings*. But the pale Danes were not the strangers who gave me a seat on the crowded train car or helped me manage the gap when I had to take my baggage on or off the train. The conductors assured me that it wasn't their job to help, but the mahogany-skinned North African immigrants riding the train had no such objection to coming to my aid.

At Copenhagen's central station, I could only detect one way to get from the train platform I had arrived at to the main terminal, where I could catch a train to the airport—down a long flight of stairs. A dark-skinned and strikingly dresses woman flashed me a brilliant smile full of pearly white teeth, sent her family down the stairs, picked up my suitcase and carry-on, and proceeded to march me down and around a path that took us, *sans* stairs, to the main station hall. At the information kiosk, she bid me safe travels and went off to reunite with her kinfolk.

Despite having missed seeing the statue incarnation of the Little Mermaid (which I have on good account is only a few feet tall and not terribly impressive), I have fond memories of my time with my niece. However, what I really treasure is the kindness of strangers I found among the immigrants who sought refuge in Denmark, and are still attuned to how difficult it is to navigate in strange countries. ■

CHAPTER PHOTO CREDIT: Walt and me in Næstved Denmark. *The Carole J. Garrison Family Archive.*

CAROLE J. GARRISON

The Næstved train station. *The Carole J. Garrison Family Archive.*

Majorie's means of transportation. *The Carole J. Garrison Family Archive.*

Church in the town center. *The Carole J. Garrison Family Archive.*

Old man sandwich shop. *The Carole J. Garrison Family Archive.*

4 Normandy

I've traveled to France frequently over the years. It's only seven hours by plane and one of my dearest friends, Beatrice, lives in a quaint village just south of Paris, a central point of departure for short forays into the tourist sites around the country. Beatrice was always my "French connection."

However, a few years ago I reconnected with another friend, Phirun, who lives in Normandy. Phirun was my first Cambodian friend in my earliest days there. She and her mother, Kim, lived only a few yards of dirt-packed alleyway down from the guesthouse where I initially stayed in Phnom Penh. They had a small kiosk in front of their dilapidated villa—a remnant of Pol Pot's destruction in the city. I remember our first meeting during one of my daily walks. She was sitting in the shop as I passed by. Our eyes met for the briefest of seconds, and then she looked down and nodded politely.

Embarrassed to be caught staring, I did a half-wave semi-bow thing. As a result, to my alarm, she waived me over to where she and her mother sat. Flustered, I had no idea what to say, having no language training beyond my fifteen important and must-know phrases for tourists in Cambodia. Still, I felt utterly compelled to grab the moment, to connect to this life and to begin living it. I snuffed out my cigarette and returned my lighter to my pocket so that I could communicate with them through hand gestures. However, Phirun could speak English and soon I was visiting their shop, and then their home, which became routine. Kim and I were close in age and came to call each other sister. True to their tradition, Phirun and her sisters treated me as their special aunt with devotion and kindness that I had rarely experienced even from my blood family.

While I hadn't seen Phirun for years, I often saw her mother and sisters on my frequent visits to Cambodia. Once I went to Normandy to visit, it became a permanent stop on any European itinerary. Visiting Phirun, as with many of the friends I see when I travel, cements relationships, and maintains an authentic human connection—whatever the connection was that originally brought us together. Coming in person to share new experiences as well as reminisce over old memories provides me a level of outlandish hospitality from most of my hosts. I would be lying if I didn't admit that I bask in that attention, especially from those who believe that their lives are linked to mine and in whose eyes I am the highest expression of myself. Why do they feel that way? Because, when we met most of these friends were in despair and/or desperation. Because of privilege, position, American citizenship or natural inclination, I was able to bring some small measure of hope, sometimes with nothing grander than a smile or a gesture of concern. And so it was with Phirun in Cambodia in 1992.

Cambodia was under French colonial rule from 1863 to 1953. Cambodians migrated to France for decades during the period of the French occupation (which greatly influenced Southeast Asia) and, more recently, after the horror of the Khmer Rouge Killing Fields.

French was practically the second language in the country until English, and then Chinese proficiency became the standard goal for upward mobility. When Phirun married a French-Cambodian national, she was able to take her young nephew to France to live with her as her son. Her elder sister was already there and likely, the matchmaker between Phirun and her twice previously divorced husband, Lykim.

Perfect, I remember thinking when I returned this time and had a toilet seat and a platter of *bahn xeo,* crispy and fragrant Asian pork pancakes, waiting for me. Phirun used my Paris arrival as an excuse to shop in Paris grocery stores for the ingredients to make my favorite dishes. I was sure roast duck would make it to the table too. Phirun had bought the new toilet seat, just for me, when my trip to Normandy had been confirmed. "I am too old," I had declared on my last visit, "to squat on cold porcelain and pee Cambodian style."

Phirun lives in a little Norman village called Vraiville. The house that she and Lykim built is a make-shift affair with rooms sprouting in all directions to accommodate their growing family. In the yard, full of construction debris from past projects or waiting for future ones, chickens scratched and a gang of noisy young roosters strutted from dawn to dusk. There were also untended gardens with flowers, a few stalks of corn, and a couple of zucchinis growing wild, along with brambles full of ripe blackberries, various and sundry vehicles, campers, hammocks, and even the odd boat or two scattered across the yard—all presided over by a venerable old black walnut tree.

Phirun had prepared her bedroom for me; she and Lykim—the children's former boxer and wanna-be Rock 'n Roller father—slept wherever they could find a flat surface in the family room. The other members of the household were Phirun's two daughters, Melodie and Emillie, stepsons Lydu (short for Ludwig), Brandon, and Chuc (really her brother's son).

As soon as I arrived at their home, I stashed my baggage on the bed and then opened the carry-on to look for the carefully chosen presents I had brought for Melodie and Emillie—a Lucky Brand tank top with a Fender guitar printed on the front for Melodie, age twelve, and a trendy top-end bracelet for her younger sister, Emillie. Melodie was thrilled and wore the shirt non-stop during my entire visit. Emillie was simply polite. Later on, I overheard her say something about dreaming of a squishy, so I returned to my bag of goodies and handed one to her. She was all smiles with squeals of joy. You would have thought that I had presented her with a new puppy. I had acquired new celebrity. *Squishies, really*, I thought. *They are dumb fifty-cent toys.* But I kept that thought private and enjoyed Emillie's gratitude.

After a bit of relaxing and enjoying Phirun's cooking, we set out to do some touristy stuff. I had already noticed the difference between this region of the country and the south-east part of France. Normandy has pretty much the opposite landscape of Provence, a region in southeastern France bordering Italy and the Mediterranean Sea, which I had visited the previous year with my pal, Beatrice. Goldenrod and mustard yellow wheat and hay fields expand over flat terrain, whereas vineyards and olive groves grow up the slopes of the Southern Alps. Lavender blooms in the cooler climes of Normandy, with a stronger fragrance closer to the ocean; but, of course, it doesn't grow in huge fields like it does in southern France. Unlike those in the Romanesque villages of Provence, the houses lining the narrow lanes that wind through these villages looked English to me, with their real and faux exterior wood beams and occasional thickly thatched roofs. But perhaps it is the Norman style that influenced the villages of England?

More touristing. With the family piled into the car, and Lydu at the wheel, we visited Normandy's ancient capital city, Rouen (pronounced *rew ah;* swallow the n) and the huge cathedral, Cathédrale Primatiale Notre-Dame de l'Assomption de Rouen, which houses the Viking king Rollo's grave. It was easy to imagine the

Vikings' long ships coming up the broad river Seine and terrifying everyone as they approached. There is a lovely monument to Joan of Arc, *sans* armor, across from the cobblestoned central plaza lined with quaint tables and umbrellas, hoping to attract the few visitors away from the less pricey McDonalds further down the street.

The old city is a tourist mecca, but the French had abandoned it during their August holidays for the beaches, so it was virtually empty. Not so for Mont St. Michel, our next stop, where we and thousands of other tourists braved ninety-plus-degree weather to climb the towering ramparts and be utterly transported back to medieval France. We were pushed with the crowd along the lowest level of the castle, down narrow winding cobblestone streets lined on both sides by small houses and shops. Above these stand the granite and limestone monastic buildings, many of which date from the thirteenth century. The higher up we climbed, the fresher the air and the less crowded were the nooks and crannies leading from one chapel to another. Any minute you could imagine a knight, in full herald regalia on horseback, come charging down the ramparts, armor glinting in the bright sun, a perfect blue sky as his backdrop.

From there we traveled to Caen and the beaches of Normandy. We walked from the simple red granite obelisk on Utah Beach to the concrete pylon paying tribute to the 5th Engineer Special Brigade Monument that overlooks Omaha Beach. The contrast between the somber memorials to the men who fought and died there in the early 1940s, and the throngs of bathers frolicking along the wide expanse of sandy beach and Atlantic surf was not lost on me. I hardly knew how to feel.

In Caen I saw groups of young African men, immigrants hoping for a chance to board a ferry to Brittany and seek asylum in England. While in Elbeof, we passed what I thought was an RV campsite right in the center of the city but, no, it was a makeshift gypsy encampment. The gypsies have apparently turned in their horses and carts for RVs and caravans. They may move about the country in a different style, but apparently their reputation for being no-goodniks remains—at least in the opinion of Lydu and his father.

The fresh air of the Normandy countryside, long walks with Phirun or one of her daughters through the village, and trips to a local recreation area to picnic and fish with the family revived me enough that most of my aches receded into mild discomfort.

On one of our walks through the village, Phirun assured me that she had long since forgiven me for my awkward matchmaking attempt to pair her with one of my staff when I worked in Cambodia back in the 1990s. Chay Kimsore, who like Phirun, was an ethnic Chinese-Khmer. Phirun's mother Kim approved of the match, but another of my employees, Ros Sopheap, unbeknownst to me, had other plans for him. Kimsore married Sopheap and Phirun immigrated to France to marry a widower her sister had found for her. I gave up matchmaking as a sideline.

Funnily, Kimsore's wife, Sopheap, had not forgiven me for my attempt to deprive her of hearts desire—until very lately. On a recent visit to Cambodia, following a marital tiff, Sopheap wondered aloud what her life would have been like had Kimsore married Phirun instead of her.

Perhaps because I was traveling with my Cambodian friends, people we met while out on a family picnic, people who didn't trace their French lineage further back than a decade, responded warmly and openly to my attempts to make conversation. Young couples let me hold their babies and nodded their approval when I knew that the black eyeliner their babies wore was to ward off evil. They invited me to sit and join them while they spoke to me in broken English about their past and hopes for the future. One Moroccan woman assured me that, if I really wanted to explore authentic Moroccan culture, I had to travel to the interior of her country, away from the popular tourist cities along the coast. Although she now resided in France, her longing for her roots was palpable.

My alarm went off at one o'clock in the morning, just minutes before the school board meeting would begin in Huntington, West Virginia—and only an hour before the roosters would welcome the day and make me wish they could all end up in a pot of chicken soup. It was my last day in Normandy. I reached for my iPad and Skyped in for the hours-long meeting. By noon I was on my way back to Palaiseau to spend the night with Beatrice before catching a plane to Istanbul. ∎

Postscript: One aspect of France which stays with me is the value put on the ancient, the antiquity, which catapults your imagination like a time machine, transporting you to a world of knights in armor riding huge desriers, great large war horses. In this world there are masked balls where yards of softly rustling silk brocades fill the senses and pageants replete with nobles draped in ermine. Then there is the very old, cared for and assuring longevity of memory beyond current history, something we don't have in the US. Finally the contemporary—an industrial signature of the 1960s—modern testaments to functionality that like in America, are devoid of any aesthetic worth.

CHAPTER PHOTO CREDIT: Outside the Historial Jeanne d'Arc in Rouen. *The Carole J. Garrison Family Archive.*

Wandering Rouen's historical center. *The Carole J. Garrison Family Archive.*

With Melodie in front of the Historial Jeanne d'Arc in Rouen. *The Carole J. Garrison Family Archive.*

Eating and enjoying Phirun's *ban xiao* (Vietnamese pancakes). *The Carole J. Garrison Family Archive.*

Emillie (l), Melodie (c), Phirun (top) and me on our fishing trip. *The Carole J. Garrison Family Archive.*

One of many World War II monuments on Normandy Beach. *The Carole J. Garrison Family Archive.*

Visiting the Cathedral in Rouen where the Viking Rollo is buried. *The Carole J. Garrison Family Archive.*

Joining the thousands of tourists at Le Mont-Saint-Michel. *The Carole J. Garrison Family Archive.*

5 Turkey

Even the travel g-ds cannot protect you from your own incompetence. I arrived at Orly in plenty of time, the midtown airport located only a short train ride from Palaiseau, the village outside of Paris where I was staying with my friend Beatrice. I sauntered up to the Pegasus Airlines counter with a fresh almond pastry in one hand and an iPad with my travel documents in the other.

I was reconciled to my decision to visit Turkey. I had promised Mahir, my former colleague who was a victim of Turkish President Erdoğan's crazed and autocratic crackdown on Western-oriented social justice professors, academicians and Western-educated police officers. I had made Istanbul a side trip on my itinerary, with flights procured through Expedia and an online visa. I checked with several Turkish friends who assured me that travel to Turkey was safe . . . for the moment, anyway.

The girl at the check-in counter squinted at my visa and looked perplexed. My Turkish online visa was valid beginning the fourteenth of August, but my ticket to Istanbul was dated the ninth. Due to my constant date changes to satisfy Beatrice's work schedule, and my inattentiveness to dates—as well as to details in general—*voila!* No flying for me! I became feverish when I could not get any help from airline personnel. They were too busy, didn't speak English, or assumed I was just another stupid American—perhaps correctly.

Agitated almost to the point of hysteria, I sat across from the departure desk and connected to the airport's Wi-Fi server. Although Pegasus Airlines claimed to have a line and website for English-speakers, I could not connect to either. Finally, an agent, a woman of color, came over to me and offered to help. A new online visa would take only minutes, and I could still catch my plane. Yep, if only I could read French. The Turkish website for its embassy in France was written only in French, and the woman who had offered to help had disappeared behind the counter. The last call for the Pegasus flight to Istanbul boomed over the loudspeaker. I ran over to the counter. A different agent shrugged and, not even looking up, said, "Too late."

Mahir was traveling hundreds of miles by bus from his home in Ankara to meet me in Istanbul, and I had to email him that I was not coming. His response conveyed disbelief and misery.

I boarded the train back to Palaiseau! It took Beatrice less than five minutes to get me a new visa for the next day on the Turkish embassy's website. She reads French. And for $600 USD, I booked a new ticket. The cost was roughly the same as my round-trip fare had been, but I could not disappoint Mahir. He had suffered too much already: prison, loss of his job as an associate professor, the documents required to get another job and, finally, a hold on his passport that made him a virtual prisoner in his own country. So, come morning, I was off again to Orly Airport and hopefully to Turkey.

Our reunion at the airport was jubilant. Mahir's cousin took on the role of chauffeur, and we didn't stop our pleasant chatter about family and friends until we had arrived at Mahir's father's house, where we would stay. "Mahir, you will tell me before I leave what happened here to you," I whispered as we got out of the car. "Yes," he replied solemnly. Then brightening, he said, "But for now, let's enjoy."

His little sister, Reyhan, covered from head to toe in a head scarf and patterned long dress, acted as hostess. A sturdy, lovely young woman who was studying Islamic theology in college, hoping to combine it with a master's degree in psychology—and a great cook—she immediately made me feel welcome. His younger brother, Faruk, was friendly and, like most eighteen-year-olds, was plugged into a phone or rummaging in the kitchen for something to eat. Mahir's father, on the other hand, looked me over silently, eschewed shaking hands, and disappeared until forced to join us for meals. Our first dinner was a lighthearted inter-rogation, Mahir setting up one Dr. Garrison story after another. Reyhan's eyes widened, Faruk laughed, the corners of Mahir's father's lips turned up occasionally at Mahir's translations, and I enjoyed my celebrity.

Since it was too early for bed, Mahir and I went for a walk in the neighborhood, strolling up narrow streets and barely avoiding getting hit by the careening traffic. Some women wore hijabs and others didn't, but nowhere did I see the black chadors or burkas of Iran and Saudi Arabia. Instead, their head scarves were brightly colored and their body covers were fashionable— and often not as modest as one might expect. Turkey had for decades been a secular country, although now the religious parties are in control. Nevertheless, with some exceptions, of course, women and men dressed as they pleased. As Mahir and I walked down a busy shopping street, I heard music blasting out of a doorway. Men were standing outside in black suits, smoking and chatting amicably. I looked questioningly from them to Mahir. "It's a Kurdish wedding," he replied to my unspoken question.

"How do you know that?"

"The music, it's not Turkish."

"Can I peek in?"

It was one of the black-suited men who answered me. "Yes, please enter. Enjoy," he said in heavily accented English, pointing to the entrance. I made my way down to a large banquet room, Mahir at my heels. We continued into a large hall, where we were pushed toward a circle of dancers as another smiling man encouraged me to join in. I demurred and took a seat at one of the tables that was pushed to the back of the room to make enough space for the dozens of swirling Kurds. The men wore dark suits; the women who weren't bundled in cloaks and headscarves wore long, conservative, ornamented dresses with silver buckles, beads, and coins glittering like mirrors as they danced with their heavily made-up faces. Dozens of Kurds were dancing in one enormous circle, a traditional folk-line dance, holding hands and working themselves up into a raucous celebration of the bride and groom.

"What are they singing?" I asked.

"I have no idea," Mahir said. "They're speaking Kurdish. Kurdish is nothing like Turkish."

On the way back to Mahir's father's home, I reflected on what I'd witnessed. A wedding like this goes on undisturbed, regardless of the political turmoil engulfing Turkey. Life comes, life goes, and the Kurds continue dancing.

Saturday was our day to be tourists, and Mahir teased that he was a special guide, a *terrorist tour guide*. It would have been funny had he not lost everything because he had been a professor and, for no other reason than teaching social justice from a Western perspective, had been put on Erdoğan's enemies list. (I was still waiting for the whole story.)

We rushed to catch the new gleaming subway to the seaport on the Bosporus. There we transferred to one of the big ferries instead of crossing to the European side of Istanbul on a metro that traveled deep under the straits. The weather was fabulous, fresh-cloudless perfect, with deep blue skies and the Istanbul skyline full of graceful minarets, in contrast to the modern skyscrapers I was used to seeing in large U.S. cities. One tram ride later and we were at the Blue Mosque with throngs of brightly clad tourists and locals enjoying the weekend and the fabled sights. Four hundred blue-shirted volunteer students wandered around with "Ask Me" printed on their shirts in different languages to help out sightseers, but they were stumped when I asked them if they could speak Khmer. We ate roasted corn—as common a treat in the East as popcorn or cotton candy is in the West. We lunched at an outdoor cafe whose photos of its food on placards at the entrance were better than the food itself. But it was a lovely setting with a great view of Hagia Sophia, the former Greek Orthodox cathedral, built in 1537 and now a museum.

Although I went to Turkey for Mahir, my one must-see was another stop at the grand bazaar. Anytime I had visited Istanbul in the past, it was never a disappointment. We wandered through only a few of its sixty covered streets and four thousand shops, taking in a kaleidoscope of colors and a medley of spicy scents, jewelry, Turkish tea sets, kilim bags, head scarves, and evil eyes. Mahir and I dressed up as a sultan and sultana for photos, giggling like schoolmates; we inspected baskets of jeweled colored spices (I still can't figure out what you do with sumac, but it's pretty), and tasted samples of Turkish delight and halvah. The rug salesmen seemed less aggressive than when I had last visited in 2013, but maybe that was because Mahir was with me. I looked less like an easy mark. Sadly for the Turks, the Turkish dollar had lost thirty percent against the euro that morning . . . a perfect time to buy a rug. I had no room for it in my small suitcase—or in my apartment, for that matter—so I passed up my chance to own an authentic Turkish carpet and hoped I would have no regrets. Mahir noted the increase in sellers who were Syrian refugees, an indication of the troubles in the Middle East and Turkey's role in them.

I took a photo in front of Hagia Sophia with a family dressed in a full spectrum of outfits: conservative covers on the mom, jeans and a long t-shirt on the teenage girl, and a bare-headed twenty-something daughter. Although I didn't know them, they were happy to include me when I asked to join them for a picture. Then, wishing me a good day, they waved Mahir and me off to continue our sight-seeing. We visited a carpet museum—a not-perfect substitute for purchasing one for myself—and saw ancient twenty-four-meter square (seventy-two square feet) carpets from the days of the sultans, when a distinctively patterned handmade carpet covered the entire floor of a nomad's tent or the walls of a prince's palace.

We sat on the all-purpose cotton scarf I had brought along in case I needed to wear it on a tour of the Blue Mosque. Because Mahir was disenchanted with the religious party currently controlling Turkey, he was reluctant to go there; so instead he led me to Gülhane Park, a lovely, hilly green full of flowers with a view of the Topkapı Palace overlooking the Bosporus. The park was crowded with young couples, dressed in both traditional and modern vibrant-colored Muslim and Western clothes, who were obviously not afraid to display affection publicly, because kissing and hugging were going on under the shade of every tree. The sheer variety of clothing (especially hijabs and long outer covers), patterns, and styles was amazing, but I was most surprised by the pedal pushers worn by many men. I had seen them on men in France, too, and I found the sight strange, maybe even effeminate, by American standards.

Of course, there were military police with big guns on horse patrol, which made both Mahir and me uncomfortable.

Mahir suggested a nap, but I insisted that he tell me about his ordeal first. And so he began a tale of authoritarianism and injustice at the hands of the Turkish government. In the days following the alleged coup in July of 2016, Mahir, along with almost all of his former students who had been sent abroad to the West for post-graduate education—ironically, by the government—were fired. Their passports were invalidated; many were arrested and jailed. Mahir, a college professor, was incarcerated a year after turning himself in. Like himself, no one he knew was involved in the coup attempt. His students' only crime was their Western education in democratic policing methods, a policy instituted by the former Turkish government in an attempt to entice the European Union to bring Turkey in as a full member. The strategy had not worked, and the current government was angry because now there was a top echelon of officers steeped in Western ideals of justice.

Turkey's president had been the choice of Mahir's father, he supported him in general elections—Erdoğan signed the order to jail his son. Needless to say, the family was in a state of trauma. There had been no communication with any of my Turkish students for months, none since those first hours of disbelief and uncertainty. I had no way to learn their fate. Then Mahir was released, and he called me on the phone. I was sitting in a hairdresser's chair when the call came. At first, we talked in a quickly generated code, not wanting to say something that might compromise his new-found freedom. Later, we found ways to communicate more freely. He lost his teaching job and supported himself washing taxi-cabs. Even if Mahir could escape Turkey, he saw no way to get his family out of the country. They were essentially under house arrest. Former friends and even family members shunned him, afraid for their own security. He and his colleagues completely lost contact.

How Mahir faces such an uncertain future with such courage is beyond comprehension. Listening to his story, I just knew that I was meant to make this trip.

Before falling asleep on my laid-out shawl, we watched some funny crow-like birds fighting futilely against the strong breeze while the sea birds floated aimlessly wherever the updrafts took them. I was a sea bird, Mahir a crow. We finally limped back to his father's house around 8:00 p.m., my toes bloody and sore from failing to wear socks.

Mahir's father's goodbye bear hug was a nice transition from his stiff, formal greeting when I first arrived. It shocked his kids to see him hug an American woman, a Jew no less, but maybe he also knew that I was meant to make the trip and give his son a connection to the outside world.■

Postscript: At the time of my trip, only one of my former Turkish students had made it out of his country, along with his wife and newborn twin girls. Somehow, they had managed to get to Greece, and from there to the States and luckily into teaching positions while they worked on their applications for asylum. Following the alleged coup, I had reached out to another student's family, whose wife and children were left behind in America when he went home to Turkey before starting a college professorship in the U.S. He cannot leave. They cannot go back. I still occasionally send money and gift boxes. It is not enough.

CHAPTER PHOTO CREDIT: Standing in front of the Hagia Sophia Museum. *The Carole J. Garrison Family Archive.*

One of the many Turkish bakery in the Sultanahmet neighborhood of Istanbul. *The Carole J. Garrison Family Archive.*

Taking in the colors and perfume at a spice shop in the Grand Bazaar. *The Carole J. Garrison Family Archive.*

Avoiding the mounted police in Gülhane Park. *The Carole J. Garrison Family Archive.*

Looking, not buying, on the rug and souvenir shopping street behind the Blue Mosque. *The Carole J. Garrison Family Archive.*

The vista across the Bosphorus Strait. *The Carole J. Garrison Family Archive.*

Photo opportunity with a family of strangers sharing the sights in Istanbul. *The Carole J. Garrison Family Archive.*

6 Palaiseau

I am a non-multilingual person, and I am definitely not French. Given the diversity of the French population (twenty-nine countries speak French), I am unable to identify the quintessential French face. Thus, anyone who speaks French is French to me, regardless of which country they come from.

Airports are just not my favorite places. I barely made the flight from Istanbul back to Paris after standing in the passport control line for close to an hour. To be honest, Mahir and I misjudged the time and spent a leisurely—too leisurely—hour drinking coffee and enjoying our last few minutes together. I was so excited feeling free and living in the moment, I did not slip into my conservative, cautious airport behavior. Now, I was paying the price. But on the positive side, while I waited in line, I saw a large group of men, clothed only in white cotton bath towels, followed by an equal number of women all wearing voluminous black burkas peeking out of narrow eye slits to see

the world. They were going on a hajj to Mecca, and the men had to dispossess themselves of all worldly possessions—although I assumed that they were wearing underpants. The entire ritual seemed similar to a concept in Buddhism that I recently learned while listening to an assortment of Great Courses on tape. These courses had helped me prepare for the second part of my journey—the part that would take me to the Tibetan Plateau and into the heart of Buddhism. The concept is that of an *anagarika*, which in Pali means homeless one, a person who has given up most or all of their worldly possessions to commit full-time to Buddhist practice (in the present case these men and women had disposed themselves of their clothing for an Islamic hajj to Mecca). Not to be disrespectful, but the men looked like a gang of seniors escaping from a Turkish bath house.

Beatrice met me at the airport, lost her car in the underground parking lot, and then took the wrong highway exit. We spent an hour or more going a twenty-minute distance, and she complained bitterly the entire trip to her place. But that's Beatrice, and any other reaction on her part would have been odd enough to cause me to think I was riding with a body snatcher.

We were scheduled to meet in Ulaanbaatar in a couple of weeks for a shared trip into the Mongolian steppes, so Beatrice was unconcerned about leaving me on my own while she went to work. Beatrice hates work. She's a civil servant in a nearby municipality, in charge of weddings and cemeteries as well as local elections. She's really an expert in electoral matters; this was how we came to know each other. Beatrice had been my partner in Cambodia when, as UN volunteers, we supervised provincial elections following the 1991 Paris Peace Accords. Sharing that intense year bonded us forever as friends, sisters, and even mother-daughter surrogates.

As I sat in Beatrice's tiny sitting room, the memory of my first meeting with Beatrice came vividly to mind. I had just landed in Cambodia to begin the mission for the United Nations (UN) and was being driven to a UN guesthouse in Phnom Penh. The van stopped at a plain, three-story cement block building with a large paved courtyard and parking lot. With little fanfare, an American volunteer—acting as a greeter for the UN's volunteer unit—announced in a cracking, occasionally squeaking voice that betrayed his youth, "New arrivals keep coming, so there is no schedule in place. Please, find something to do." As there was no more information forthcoming, a female staffer led me to my room.

"You have a roommate, Beatrice," she said. Conspiratorially, she added, "Beatrice is from France and, between you and me, she's a *bit* difficult. I hope you will manage."

Tired and more apprehensive—teenage boys staffing HQ and a bit difficult French woman—I stepped into a white-washed cement room bereft of personality, the two twin beds taking up most of its space. On the single bureau, a small silver-framed photo of an elderly man and a plum-colored glass bottle of perfume were the only signs of Beatrice's occupancy.

Two large windows opened onto a balcony that overlooked the courtyard and a three-story, bombed-out office building across the way, with many of its walls missing or partially destroyed. An open door beyond the beds revealed a Western-style bathroom. As I was considering a shower and a nap, my roommate came through the door, pushing my luggage out of her way.

Unsmiling, a young, slightly built woman stared at me from intense brown eyes set in an olive complexion, her skin so pale it looked as if it rarely saw the sun. Short, softly curled auburn hair framed her narrow, serious face. *"Bonjour,"* she said her voice a flat monotone. Not even a hint of welcome accompanied the greeting.

"Parlez-vous English?" I asked hopefully.

"Oui," she replied, her dark eyes holding my gaze. "I have traveled in America, but I prefer to speak French."

◻◉◻

Palaiseau is a village located close to the southern end of the Paris suburban train line. The first morning that I walked to the village center to get a fresh baguette, the *patisserie*, as well as most of the shops, were locked up tighter than a drum. Although I shouldn't have been surprised, among those shuttered establishments were the communist and socialist party headquarters—not something you would normally see on an American shopping street. Tempting lemon and fruit tarts, creamy quiches, and chocolate éclairs—along with satisfying my curiosity about France's left-wing political parties—would have to wait for another day, since I'd forgotten about the regular Monday closings. So I walked aimlessly, turning my attention to the cobblestone streets and hidden courtyards. They were old, quaint, and shabby, but I knew from the ride in from the airport that the surrounding environs of Palaiseau were new, modern, and ugly. Then I headed back to Beatrice's cottage because, despite believing that one should never wait for moments to happen, and that life must be experienced, I chose to experience waiting for Beatrice to come home. Besides, my head felt three sizes too small for my brain, and I needed to rest.

After twenty-plus years of visiting Beatrice in France, I had finally mastered the trains from Palaiseau to Paris; but not so much the metro in the city. No matter. One morning I got on a train and headed to Paris to visit the Louvre. It was closed on Tuesday—of course it was! All the major art museums were closed. I took photos outside the museum and got in on a professional shoot of two lovers, a scene highlighting Paris as the City of Love. I snapped pics of the Eiffel Tower, the Arc de Triomphe, and Joan of Arc's statue in front of the Deauville Hotel on the Champs Elysees. In my viewfinder, the Eiffel Tower replaced the minarets of Istanbul, and the ubiquitous Parisian neck scarves replaced the ever-present head scarves of Turkey.

I headed for Angelina's, the Paris restaurant most famous for melted chocolate with whipped cream. There was no line (usually the wait was an hour or more), and I was seated immediately. As I sipped and savored my cup of hot chocolate, I forgot all about the closed museums. Tuesday was a good day.

I left the restaurant to walk (hoping to burn up a few calories) in search of the Jewish quarter and the Agoudas Hakehilos synagogue, but I never found them. Despite this disappointment, I did find the memorial and gravesite of Louis XVI and Marie Antoinette, at St. Denis Basilica where I had never been before. Ah, all who wander are not lost! They just end up in different places.

Beatrice and I spent our few evenings together under handmade quilts—lap blankets—that I had made for her over the years from bits of material I was always collecting on my journeys. We watched television until our eyes were too heavy to keep open. Beatrice prepared a hot water bottle for me to relieve the arthritis in my chest, and it was lights out by ten o'clock or earlier.

Beatrice took me to the airport to catch the flight to Moscow, complaining the whole way there, although she felt strongly that she had to see me off. Perhaps she was afraid that I would have another airport mishap, and would find me back at her front door. There were no tearful *"au revoir,"* only "See you in Ulaanbaatar." ∎

CHAPTER PHOTO CREDIT: Enjoying a cup of hot chocolate Angelina's Paris tea room. *The Carole J. Garrison Family Archive.*

Locked out of the Musée du Louvre. *The Carole J. Garrison Family Archive.*

Looking for the temple in the Jewish quarter of Paris. *The Carole J. Garrison Family Archive.*

Paris view with the Eifel tower across the Seine River. *The Carole J. Garrison Family Archive.*

The memorial and gravesite of Louis XVI and Marie Antoinette, at St. Denis Basilica in Paris. *The Carole J. Garrison Family Archive.*

Musée de l'Orangerie. *The Carole J. Garrison Family Archive.*

Paris is for lovers. *The Carole J. Garrison Family Archive.*

7 Moscow

My shocking pink carry-on bag was considerably lighter by the time I arrived in Moscow, having belatedly delivered Beatrice's birthday and Christmas presents—postage is expensive from the States to Europe, so I decided to bring them myself. The gifts for Slava and his wife, Sveta, were considerably smaller—fridge magnets from places I had just visited to add to their collection of hundreds, and a little change purse for Sveta. Slava, like Phirun and Beatrice, was also a friend from the year I worked as an Electoral Supervisor for the United Nations in Cambodia. I couldn't fly over Russia without dropping by.

"*Zdravstvute.*" Slava greeted me with smiles and a traditional Russian bear hug. It wasn't too bad since he was still painfully thin. Narrow-faced and a little grayer than I remembered, Slava's time with the Russian military in Afghanistan had prematurely aged him even before we met in 1992. His spectacles

over his gray eyes made him look like a starving poet or a writer from Dostoevsky's time. His English, less thickly accented after years of working for the U. S. Drug Enforcement Administration (DEA) in Moscow, still had an ironic twist and a sly humor that belied his ever-present depression—a depression exacerbated by recent dismissals of Russian employees by U.S. agencies due to the political machinations of our two governments.

It took a while in Moscow traffic to get home to his 1950s apartment block on the broad, tree-lined Leninsky Prospekt, where he and Sveta lived with their tiny dog in a tiny newly renovated one-bedroom apartment.

The drive gave me the opportunity to transport myself back some twenty-five years ago. I met Slava when Beatrice and I moved from Phnom Penh to a rural village in the province of Kampong Cham. He was part of the UN's military team assigned to the area. I shared my Russian and Ukrainian origins with him and to his delight, practiced some of my rusty college Russian, which consisted of little more than *krasnaya sabaca* (red dog) and *nyet* (no).

Like many Eastern Europeans I met during the mission, Slava tried to reconcile his demons through western music. It was no wonder that Freddy Mercury's song, "What Are We Living For?" had such a powerful effect on him. He had come from dark places. He had spent a terrifying stint in Afghanistan with the KGB and was trying to reclaim his place in the world, in order to make up for lost years, and to grab hold of some sort of gold ring. Now temporarily free of the Soviet yoke, Slava had begun to develop an appetite for life, freedom and adventure. I became a trusted part of that adventure.

No matter where I was, I managed to preserve my ritual of drinking coffee, and doing neck exercises and a brief meditation in the dark of early morning. It was always early morning, either because I was fatigued from jet lag or had gone to bed by eight o'clock the previous evening, not wanting to venture out at night alone. I kept a stash of instant coffee with me, and if all else failed, Folgers sustained me. I would then pop a few Aleve, but pain relief became less and less a part of my ritual as the journey progressed. Like my maternal grandmother, Bertha, if I had something to do, all thoughts of minor discomfort faded like the morning dew on a summer's day. By the time I reached Moscow, the debilitating arthritis was receding, and all my strategies were working: knee bands, wrist bands, and a trick I learned from Sveta—a rolled towel under my neck to sleep. I had expandable walking sticks, too, but they were tucked away in the suitcase unused, save for a few long walks in Normandy.

It didn't take long to come to the conclusion that Moscow was not the dirty, drab city with long bread lines and no flowers that I had first visited in the frigid winter of 1993. It was vibrant, with clean broad avenues, and full of late-model cars of every kind, as well as large shady parks, ponds, and stores as expensive and fancy as Whole Foods and Trader Joe's. The famous GUM (pronounced *guum*) department store had become a five-star mall, with multiple lobbies and floors that could compete with Rodeo Drive for most ostentatious merchandise and decor. I could hardly afford its famous ice cream cones.

Although public transportation was new and efficient, the old metro was still a place of magnificent Soviet-era sculpture and the longest, steepest escalators on the planet. All the other sculptures in Moscow had been moved to Gorky Park to guard the entrance to Red Square. If you look past the onion domes of the iconic St. Basil's Cathedral, and the looming statute of Peter the Great, you can see a modern cityscape of new skyscrapers worthy of any large metropolis in the world. But what caught my eye and interest was the pre-War World II architecture, the gleaming gold-tipped churches, and the endless gingerbread decorating every building.

Anar, a former Criminal Justice graduate student, one of several recruited from Russia, an ethnic Azerbaijani living in Moscow, arranged to spend a day with me. The day with Anar was charming. He was generous, attentive and eager to treat his old professor with great deal of courtesy and hospitality. Now married with children, he no longer looked like an "Islamic terrorist." When he was my student in the post 9/11 era, he was lean, with a shaved head. Although he was as far from a terrorist as anyone could be, he set off alarm bells every time he went to an airport. I remember counseling him to keep his temper in check when security personnel subjected him to additional precautionary measures.

Anar and I communicated several times since he graduated in 2010 and returned to Moscow. A few emails about job opportunities, family news and once I put he and Slava together in hopes that Slava might know of any prospects Anar could follow up with. I was the beneficiary of Anar's time in America.

Anar knew I wanted to visit funky museum that was celebrating my favorite book, *The Master and Margarita* (1967), chosen one of the hundred best novels in the world in the twentieth century. In the novel, the devil, Woland, and his cronies arrive in Soviet-era Moscow and pandemonium ensues. Far more compelling than the fantasy and satire was what I interpreted to be the best argument for a belief in g-d. Bulgakov's treatment of good and evil is less of a struggle and more like two sides of the same coin, where one cannot exist without the other. *I have no doubt that evil exists in the world, so maybe g-d does as well.* Anar and I climbed the narrow, graffiti-covered stairwell to the Stalin-era apartment of author Mikhail Bulgakov. I joined the ranks of other visitors; pilgrims who were paying homage to this literary masterpiece of fiction, fantasy, and satire. Read the book. Visit the museum.

My reverence for the book had another, a more secret motivation, than just acknowledging the novels literary value, something that Anar and I did share. My secret had to do with my introduction to it, many years before on a mountaintop in Cambodia. I was with my Polish major, a UN military observer stationed in the province I was assigned to work. We were not yet lovers, but headed inexorably in that direction. Prior to our mountaintop tryst our conversations were strangers-to-friends bridges, which we used as a mechanism for taking each other's measure. That night we shared ideas about books and poetry, as if they were gifts or as surrogates for physical pleasure. Excited, he told me about *The Master and Margarita*—a Soviet-era novel that weaves together satire and realism, art and religion, as well as history and contemporary social values. But for Stephan, the narrative was a magical tale of true love, witchcraft and redemption. "Can you try to find this book?" he asked. "Together we will read and share this wonderful story."

Share, yes, I thought. Stephan wanted to share something—not something that we had brought with us, but something that we discovered together. And so did I.

My love affair with Stephan ended when we concluded the mission, but not my attachment to the novel and its connection to him. Visiting the museum for me was a way of reliving that bit of "true love" in my own life.

From there we went to the famed Tretyakov Gallery to see classical Russian art. Anar made a good docent. For months he had taken his young son there for art classes, and he knew the entire collection. After viewing paintings of Russian fairytales, I found myself compelled to buy a pricey lacquer box depicting a scene from the tale titled "Prince Ivan, the Firebird, and the Gray Wolf." After the museum, we checked out a Viking festival that stretched for blocks along Garden

Blvd. The festival was buzzing with tourists and Muscovites enjoying the weather, the Viking-era games, and tents full of axes and horned helmets for sale.

Anar drove me around to some of the standard tourist sights and shared some Russian trivia. *Bolshoi* does not mean ballet; it means "big theater," and the Bolshoi sits next to the little theater. Both were painted canary yellow and decorated with what looked to me like white icing. We drove past two of the most prominent of the seven sisters, Stalin-era skyscrapers: the former KGB headquarters, now the Foreign Affairs building, and its matching apartment building where Stalin housed all his friends—those who lived with lavish privileges despite their supposedly classless society. Anar and I shared a laugh as we imagined the gossip, perhaps fear, which would ensue when an apartment became available. I felt again the power and the draw of Bulgakov's novel. He had created a zany version of Moscow, a chaotic place controlled by a force of unaccountable, capricious power. People had no agency or control over their fate and, like those who displeased Stalin, could disappear for no apparent reason.

By the time Anar deposited me back at Slava's apartment block, I had traversed most of Moscow's tourist sites, enjoyed a rare and sweet reunion with a former student, and felt wholly compensated for the aggravating and expensive process of getting a Russian visa in the era of Trump-Putin shenanigans.

Slava and I walked nearly everywhere and, by the third day, I had already walked the equivalent of a marathon. Slava kept me walking, more so to sneak a cigarette than to help me exercise to reduce my arthritis pain. He was anxious about a new job offer that had political overtones, which would be very different from his prior work as a translator for the U.S. DEA in Russia. He had lost that job as a consequence of one of Trump's pretend crackdowns on Russian misbehavior. And his wife pretended not to notice his attempt to keep his smoking a secret. She confided that he was always apprehensive when he felt uncertain or insecure about what lay ahead, but she wasn't concerned. "Once he's on the job, he'll be fine. He's always like this," Sveta said. She smiled and continued to cook all my favorite traditional Russian dishes—blinis, roast tongue, borsht. They were all things that my Ukrainian-born grandmother had made for me when I was young. Sitting at their tiny table in their narrow kitchen, my mouth stuffed full, I was transported back sixty years or more to my grandmother's kitchen, where I stood in line behind brothers and cousins to get a hot blini—a thin, unfilled crepe that we called a "blinskin."

Slava and Sveta were wonderful hosts, and Moscow had been a treat. I was quite sure that Trump had done nothing to damage the Russian bear, only common Russians who unfortunately had worked for U.S. agencies in Moscow. I was worn out. Ulaanbaatar was my next stop and my first trip into this unknown territory, which I hoped would put me on the path of the Buddha. ∎

CHAPTER PHOTO CREDIT: Standing with the Devils companions in front of The Bulgakov House, Bolshaya Sadovaya Street, Moscow. *The Carole J. Garrison Family Archive.*

Shopping for Matryoshka dolls. *The Carole J. Garrison Family Archive.*

Checking out Museum Park outside the Kremlin. *The Carole J. Garrison Family Archive.*

Walking down Sveta's favorite old street of Russian Churches. *The Carole J. Garrison Family Archive.*

8 Mongolia

Sain Uu is how you say "hello" in Mongolian.

The round, portable white tents called *yurts* (from the Turkic languages), referred to as *gers* by the locals, sprouted like mushrooms dotting the Mongolian steppes and the yards and terraces of Ulaanbaatar, where the new media celebrity of Chinggis Khan, (more widely known as Ghengis Khan), had become a national marketing ploy. It had certainly worked on me! After watching *Marco Polo* on Netflix, the acclaimed movie Mongol and most recently, the documentary, *The Eagle Huntress,* I was obsessed with visiting Mongolia. It, along with Bhutan, were definitely on my bucket list to see before arthritis crippled me.

The landscape from the plane as it landed looked like the Dakota Badlands. A pall of pollution hung over the city, which I later learned was the result of everyone returning from summer holidays. The sky bridge from the plane to the airport terminal smelled decidedly of sheep dung, but passport control and

finding a cab was easy. After having only three hours' sleep, I needed "easy."

Mongolia is six hours ahead of Moscow so, even though I was seriously sleep-deprived, it was too early for bedtime.

Mongolia was the beginning of phase two of my travel plans, the time I would discover new friends and new places. With that in mind, long before I left the U.S., I was in contact with the Short Tours travel agency in Mongolia. Beatrice and I wanted a three-day tour out on Mongolia's steppes, but first I needed a few days to myself in Ulaanbaatar, Mongolia's capital city. I desired to do some volunteer work on this trip, needing to create a little good karma to make up for the exorbitant investment I was making to indulge my fantasies. (I had recently been studying religions of the Axial age and more specifically Buddhism by listening to *Great Courses* CDs in my car, so I knew that I would be iclose to the heart and soul of Tibetan Buddhism—the perfect place, I reasoned, to earn some karma points.)

After not getting anywhere on my own, I asked Urnaa, the contact at the tour agency, for help. "I don't know if you are in Ulaanbaatar, but I would like to spend an afternoon or two teaching conversational English at a community center or school. I wrote to the U.S. Embassy and to the Buddhist cultural center to see if I could volunteer, but I have not heard back from anyone. Do you know whom I might contact?"

Urnaa replied, "In Mongolia, the summer vacation for schoolchildren is from June to September. Also, most people take their vacations and come back in

September. At the time of your arrival, they will be busy preparing for the start of school, but I will ask my acquaintances about it."

By the time I arrived in country, Urnaa had not yet confirmed any volunteer opportunities. So I emailed her from the hotel, hoping she had something lined up. We agreed to meet in the afternoon.

"There's a bridge right on the river; let's meet on the bridge," she texted to my iPad. "The bridge is known as Lion Bridge (*Арслантай sуур* in Mongolian), and everyone knows it. P.S. I am wearing a black dress with flowers and have shoulder-length hair." To which I replied, "See you there. I have on blue print pants and a pink shirt. Short hair."

After a quick shower, I arranged with the desk clerk for a city tour the next day, borrowed an umbrella setting out in the rain to find my bearings, scope out the surroundings, and meet Urnaa. My first stop was a Korean shopping mall, whose floor plan and customer traffic flow defied comprehension. To reach the grocery store, you have to go up one floor, make your way to the back of a Walmart-like general store, and take an escalator back down to the grocery store. It took several tries and lots of futile attempts to communicate with the guards who blocked the entrance before I managed to find my way to the groceries. I bought some familiar-looking items for the fridge in my hotel room—juice, a pre-mixed salad, and some cookies. From the restaurant signs in the mall's food court, it was obvious that Mongolians enjoy a Russian-style black burger, made with black bread buns and served at the local Burger King.

Back on the street, I passed several large KFCs. I joked later in an email home that maybe they were franchises financed by drug lords, similar to the drug tunnel that had just been discovered in the U.S. running under a KFC to Mexico. I could see Soviet-style apartment blocks everywhere—left over, I later learned from Urnaa, from the communist post-World War II era, built by Russian soldiers. "Actually," Urnaa had said, "they are quite coveted for their superior construction compared to current apartment buildings." They were exactly like the apartment block I had just stayed in while in Moscow.

From the intense traffic, it seemed that every Mongolian must own a car, and that each one of them was a universally bad driver. Mongolians drive on crowded streets, laying on their horns, and they drive on sidewalks. Motorists fail to embrace the concept of stopping for pedestrians at crosswalks, and the city fathers had failed to clean the rubbish from the pedestrian tunnels constructed under broad, heavily congested streets. However, the hawkers were out in full force, especially those with stocks of umbrellas to sell. On a positive note, most Mongolians drive slowly, so traffic fatalities are low.

I did a day's worth of walking despite the deluge, avoiding deep puddles from the incessant rain that was overwhelming Ulaanbaatar's sewer system— unprepared, I learned later, for the unusually heavy rains. They were the consequence, most Mongolians I met believed, of global warming. (Menacingly, the Gobi Desert was flooding during my stay.) After a trek to Chinggis Khan Square, renamed in 2016 due to the focus on the Khan's new notoriety, and an opportunistic photo shoot in front of a ninety-fifth anniversary celebration of Mongolia's famed poet, Natsagdorj Dashdrji (whose statute replaced Lenin's after Mongolia's democratic revolution in the early 1990s), I set off to meet Urnaa on the Lion Bridge. Not only was I unsure how to find the Lion Bridge, asking every other passerby for directions, but I wasn't sure I'd recognize her when I got there. It should be noted that the vast majority of Mongolian women have mid-length to long black hair and wear black clothing.

Not surprisingly, she spotted me first, came across the intersection, and hugged me. We scurried out of the rain to a small coffee shop and talked like old friends catching up after a long separation. Urnaa was in her early twenties, personable, fluent in English, and up on Mongolian history and current events; we bonded as easily as two people who find out they are long-lost aunt and niece. She had arranged for me to meet several newly graduated English language teachers, and she was working to arrange my visit to a private K-12 school that was already open for the school year. Her aunt was an administrator there, and Urnaa hoped she could pull some strings.

Back at the hotel before I passed out from jet lag, I sat in my room flipping through television news from all over the world. I was no longer depressed only by U.S. news reports; I could be disheartened in multiple languages and by numerous self-interests. Most broadcasts were Fox News look-alikes. When

Urnaa and I had been together earlier, she revealed that most American tourists she had met described President Trump as deplorable; however, although she didn't think he was a decent leader—much less a good man—she confided that Mongolia's more serious problem was China. "China wants to control and own all," she said, displaying more than a little hostility in her delivery. It was good to get a different perspective.

It rained all night and was still overcast when I woke, but I got up early and dressed, looking forward to my one-person city tour. No one but me and a guide. Beatrice wouldn't arrive until the next day. Then came a knock on the door. Beatrice, tired and a bedraggled, stood waiting to come in.

"You're here," I said. It was not quite a question, nor an explanation. I looked at her blankly and she stared back, her eyes squinting and a scowl blossoming across her face.

"Of course I'm here. I was to arrive today."

"Crap," I thought, taking one of her bags and giving her a wan smile. *I was wondering how I could mix up so many dates.*

"Well," I said, trying to think how to salvage my plans rather than attempt to renegotiate them with Beatrice. "Surely you need to rest. I will leave you to recover from the flight from Paris and see you later." Before she could object, I was out the door and on my way to the lobby.

It would be tedious to recount, or for anyone to read, every bit of information I soaked up that day with the young man who guided me through Ulaanbaatar's treasures. He explained that the syllable "om" was used in meditation because everyone, including a mute, could make the sound. Other odd tidbits included the fact that Mongolian male wrestlers wear open-front vests to show their gender, lest they be beaten in a match by a woman; that the huge statute in Chinggis Khan Square does not depict the famous Mongol conqueror but rather Sükhbaatar, founder of Ulaanbaatar; and that the three Buddhist temples in the city were left unharmed by the Russians so that the dictator, Stalin, could convince a visiting U.S. vice president that he was allowing religious tolerance while occupying the country.

I picked up another interesting fact in a museum gallery of traditional Mongolian clothes that displayed costumes with ridiculously long, flowing sleeves from the Manchurian Qing Dynasty era of the seventeenth and eighteenth centuries. According to my guide, the sleeves were designed so that women could hide their babies from Manchurian authorities. He also told me that coal was a major industry and, yes, that black lung disease was as rampant as smoking—a familiar malady in my current home state of West Virginia.

What I found most interesting was the back story of Mongolia's current political reality. During World War II, when the Japanese were threatening to move west across Mongolia and menace Russia, the Russians protected the Mongolians from the Japanese. However, not too many years later, the Mongolians had to save themselves from the Russians.

The day I departed Moscow, I received an email with awful news. My colleague and dear friend from Kentucky, Victor, suffered an aneurysm and was in dire condition. I was now at the portal of Tibetan Buddhism. I was compelled to embrace this deep sense of aliveness and interconnectedness I had in this place and time. In this moment I surrendered myself to the universality of Buddhist thought and tradition—as I understood it—in a heartfelt attempt to aid in Victor's recovery. Every temple had an ample supply of prayer wheels, which, if I rolled them counter-clockwise to invoke the powerful, attention and blessings of Chenrezig, the embodiment of compassion, would aid Victor's health. My guide and I, at the temple housing the one hundred and twelve foot high statue of Megjid Janraisag, dutifully rolled at least a hundred prayer wheels.

As I ran my hands along the lines of prayer wheels, I considered how Victor became so dear to me that he became a primary inspiration of my journey. Certainly, it was more appropriate to focus on his recovery than asking for my own remission—too selfish. I remembered one of our first meetings as department chair. Victor was a senior faculty member, a well-published and prominent scholar—a big brain. He was also an informal leader of one faction of a split department, one that torn apart with animosities and a deep intellectual divide. I was hired to heal the rift, each side having their own expectations of how that was to happen. I was in his office promoting my ideas for uniting the faculty prior to a departmental meeting. I laughed aloud when I remembered the one thing we did agree on—providing a good lunch at the meeting would keep blood levels down and reduce tensions. Unfortunately, that was all we agreed to.

I left his office, not remembering the details of our discussion but only his final words thundering in my head, "that would be a deal breaker." It was a threat to his cooperation. Years later when I would remind him of those words, he would beg me to forget them and "let go of the past." I had let go and Victor became my sounding board, my rabbi, my chief strategist. He was an academic socialist, bolstered by study and intellect—I was a red-diaper baby, raised by an eastern-European refugee whose Bolshevik relatives paid for their revolution with their lives.

Victor and I shared another similarity; we had both been police officers prior to becoming academics, we had both experienced descending into and escaping the heart of darkness that accompanies wearing a gun. We had bonded in a mutual desire to reform policing. He wrote the police ethics textbooks, I taught the classes. Together we influenced students like Anar and created disciples. Together we energized the department until it became an internationally recognized Criminal Justice program—a program I bequeathed to him when I retired.

My efforts on behalf of my friend continued inside the prayer hall. I inhaled incense by wafting the fumes three times toward me, the same way Shabbat candles are lit; and, at the entrance to the palace of Bogd Khan, the last of Mongolia's political/religious leaders, I beseeched the four Buddhist deities of death to rescue Victor.

The day ended with a typical tourist attraction, a traditional dance and song performance, with an unexpected and mesmerizing act—Mongolian throat singers whose sounds were a mix of throaty-hoarse chanting and deep growling. It was other-worldly, spiritual, and very animalistic all at the same time. After the show, refreshed and excited from hearing the throat singers, I stopped to pick up some yak leather souvenir wallets and then eagerly went back to the hotel to find a rested and waiting Beatrice.

We had another two days before we set out for the grasslands that stretched endlessly before the Altai Mountains. Together, Beatrice and I explored other areas of the city. We went to museums—Beatrice was not as fond of visiting monasteries and temples as I was—and we learned a few useful Mongolian words: *bayarlalaa*, meaning "thank you" (pronounced bayarlach by many) and *bayartti,* meaning "goodbye" (pronounced bayertech). These words sounded a lot like Klingon in *Star Trek.* I found myself saying goodbye a lot when I meant to say thank you.

I left Beatrice to visit some of the sites I had seen on my tour while I chatted with four English language students who had recently graduated; all planned to teach, and a few were also aspiring writers. I gifted them with a small bit of career advice while thoroughly enjoying their company and attention. Beatrice and I parted company one more time when Urnaa took me to the private high school. There I met with dozens of high school juniors, all earnestly seeking advice on how to get into the most prestigious universities in the world. These kids wanted to go to Harvard, Oxford, and MIT; any lesser school would be a drastic disappointment to their parents and their own self-image. They were eager, polite, and funny. When it was time to leave, I passed out all the squishies I had brought along, which were not enough for everyone. I watched the kids come to blows and tears over trying to get one for themselves. I was amused that the teacher asked for two to take home to her children. Squishies are a global phenomenon.

To be sure, an account of my journey to Mongolia's countryside should be a separate chapter, or at least a part two of this one. Mongolia outside of Ulaanbaatar is a world unto itself. You can see golden eagles circling an empty sky as often as you would see a turkey buzzard in Kentucky, but you won't see any people, organized villages, or paved roads. Mongolia's capital is a congested, polluted city; but once Beatrice and I left for the vast open green terrain of the steppes, we were in another world.

I doubt that a society attempting to keep its soul and culture while moving forward economically is remotely possible.

Although we traveled only fifty miles or so outside of Ulaanbaatar, it was enough to envision the vastness of the Mongolian steppes. And since there are no signs and little to guide you except for GPS (for those who have the technology) or the stars (for those who can navigate by them), it is probably better not to venture too far. The expanse of Mongolia's country-side lifted our spirits as we left behind the congested city. Despite it being late August, the air was fresh and crisp, and the few clouds in the seemingly infinite blue sky scuttled quickly across the horizon.

On the road that led out of Ulaanbaatar, we drove past small villages that looked like refugee camps with dilapidated buildings, old cars and trucks, fences, and the occasional *ger*— places the nomads stayed when they had to leave the countryside to seek shelter from the weather. As we got further away from the city, the landscape became emptier of signs of civilization, and the road became narrower until we were driving on dirt tracks. Instead of villages, we saw small clusters of white gers spread out miles apart. We drove past herds of yak, cows, horses, and sheep. Close to the road were small shaman cairns— piles of stone around a wood post, tied with ribbons; at the larger ones, there were souvenir sellers as well as camels and eagles tethered and waiting to be photographed by tourists or, more specifically, us. Beatrice and I walked clockwise three times around one shamanic marker and, as instructed, threw three rocks onto the pile. We too wanted a safe journey and, to Beatrice, shaman-ism was much more fascinating than Buddhism.

We slept in a ger camp that provided a central shower and a toilet cabin for the thirty-odd gers on the prem-ises. Our ger, about fifty feet uphill from the shower/toilet facility, was not going to service my nocturnal potty needs when temperatures were dropping into the teens at night. Our young guide, Buya, worked some magic, and I was given a self-contained toilet, like babies use. (For more money, we could have stayed in a camp with more amenities, including indoor plumbing.) There was a wood-burning stove in the center of the tent, which boiled us when the stove was lit and froze us when it wasn't. We were in ger number thirty-three, although our key said thirty-one; staying in the camp was like that—not quite correct. Dinner was something other than what was posted on the menu, and stoves were relit at 4:00 a.m. with all the noise of an elephant stampede.

On our outings outside the camp, we visited a nomad family and passed out squishies to the kids, cautioning the children not to eat them like marshmallows. We ate yak butter-cheese and bread, which I consumed with gusto, washed down with Mongolian tea. (I am a long-time admirer of Mongolian tea). Beatrice demurred, explaining that yak butter-cheese is too rich for her; she merely pushed around the bits of yak fat floating on top of her cup of tea, rather than drinking it. We also roamed the countryside looking for a variety of real or re-imagined military camps, schools, temples, and palaces which, when found, transported us palpably to the era of Chinggis Kahn.

Twenty-five percent of Mongolians practice shamanism so, to Bea's delight, some shaman camps were still in operation. In a large shaman camp, hundreds of years old, we peeked into men's tents filled with weaponry and visited women's tents dedicated to fertility. We stopped at the cave where, according to the story, one hundred monks hid for three days to escape the Chinese communists who were trying to eradicate Mongolia's religious order. Maybe the most interesting sight was a turtle-shaped rock aptly called Turtle Rock. The rock itself, large but marginally impressive, was not what caught my attention. No, it was the CCTV camera pointed at the rock to capture any mischief-makers or would-be graffiti artists in action. In the words of the controversial English artist, Banksy, "One world under CCTV."

One evening our English-speaking guide, a self-described country man, entertained us with delightful personal stories about his challenging nomadic life on the steppes, the grassland plains without trees. My favorite stories were those about him and his grandfather, a cunning and wise teacher, who was the perfect companion for an impetuous and reckless little boy. Eyes twinkling, Buya told us this story:

"Ovoo, Grandfather, I want to hunt a bear."

"You are too young, and the bear is too dangerous."

"No, Ovoo, I can do it. You take me to hunt the bear."

Granddad shrugged, took a long pull off his pipe, and shook his head to indicate "yes." My granddad was silent, rough, and stern. He was a widower, and my mum was widowed as well. He lived with us, and he often took charge of my training.

My grandfather and I set out into the hills and eventually entered a large cave. I heard a low grumbling sound before I saw it. The bear was asleep. I tugged at grandfather's sleeve; I danced around like I had to pee. "Let's go," I whispered, desperate to get away from the sleeping monster.

"But you wanted to hunt the bear. Here is the bear. We do not go."

"Please, granddad. I'm only little, and the bear is big."

Grandfather waited, an eternity, I think, and finally turned toward the cave entrance and strode out, with me in his wake.

Over the few days, Buya told us about getting lost in the Gobi; his romance with the daughter of a wealthy businessman and the father's attempt to bribe him to stay away; his effort to produce a record album of traditional Mongolian music; and his role as a bad guy in a movie that would be filmed in the fall.

On the way back to Ulaanbaatar on our last morning of the tour, we stopped at the recently built Chinggis Kahn Park. An epic statue one hundred and forty-one feet high, a museum, an art gallery, a café, and souvenir shops all awaited eager tourists. Although I won't describe the park in detail, I'm sure that tourists can't avoid a stop there—and to be fair, it was well done.

Back at the hotel, I woke with Montezuma's revenge, which lasted all day; and Beatrice was throwing up. Adding to her misery, she feared that she would miss her upcoming tour to the Gobi Desert. I drank smart water and wondered if I'd make my plane to

Xining, China, the next morning. I was grateful, however, that we weren't sick the previous night in the ger; it would have been a disaster with my little potty chair. *I must have enjoyed the yak butter too much!* We spent the day and night in bed, except for a brief foray—despite both of us being dizzy and weak—to the small Zanabazar Museum of Fine Art, brimming with exquisite examples of perfect Buddhas and Buddhist paintings, which I refused to miss.

Beatrice had complained about the cold, complained about my being busy the day she arrived, and that I abandoned her midway through her holiday, leaving her to go to the Gobi alone. She hated the local food, didn't enjoy the monasteries, and carped about an article she had read about Mongolian men treating their women badly. Nevertheless, Beatrice's email a few weeks later thanked me for our time in Mongolia. "The trip would not have happened except for your going," she wrote. "It was my best adventure in decades. Where do we travel next year?" ∎

Postscript: For those with Mongolia on their bucket list, the best way to describe the country is it's like fine wine that blends Tibetan and Korean influences, with a cover of Russian and Manchurian flavors. So for those of you who dream of visiting Mongolia, go. Arrive in June for the big festivals and crowds, or go when we did—late in August, before the first snow.

CHAPTER PHOTO CREDIT: Posing with a Chinggis Khan warrior and imagining life on the Mongolian steppes. (Historians of the Mongol empire generally prefer this spelling as opposed to Genghis Khan.) *The Carole J. Garrison Family Archive.*

Watching, not riding, the camels on display for tourists headed out to the steppes. *The Carole J. Garrison Family Archive.*

Posing with a Mongolian artist who paints on leather after my guide shamed me into buying one of his paintings. *The Carole J. Garrison Family Archive.*

Mugging it at a small city museum in Ulaanbaatar. *The Carole J. Garrison Family Archive.*

Dreaming of being an Eagle Huntress. *The Carole J. Garrison Family Archive.*

Standing before a throne in the Bogd Khan Palace Museum. *The Carole J. Garrison Family Archive.*

9 Xining, China

I woke up in Xining, China, a city going through rapid—some might say rabid—modernization. From a backwater town on the edge of the Tibetan plateau, it was becoming the Eastern gate of the Qinghai-Tibet Plateau. I had picked it precisely for its close proximity to ancient Tibet. Other than that, I had no clue about my location except that I was in a small Chinese hotel with almost no Western amenities. The staff did not speak English, and they were horrified when I showed up at 9:00 p.m. "claiming" to have a reservation.

I was equally confounded when, via a translation app on the desk clerk's phone, the hotel assured me that it had no business association with Expedia, and thus I had no reservation. No reservation; never heard of Expedia; no prepaid room; no English spoken. I didn't exactly cry, but I didn't smile either. In a masterful communication effort, with the help of the receptionist's translation app, I got a room and

negotiated Expedia's rate (asking my daughter to deal with the confusion), to be paid with cash only. No foreign credit cards accepted. On a roll, I requested a non-smoking room. Someone sprayed it with canned air freshener and called it "good." I piled the comforters and blankets on the uncomfortable bed, which was still hard as a rock, and I was instructed to boil the water before drinking it. Oh, and I was told that I could not access Google in China. Before going to my room, I emailed my son-in-law to request that he send me a Googled list of the ten best things to do in Xining.

I lay in bed the first morning, remembering my initial bouts with post-shingles maladies, when I had slept on a rock-hard bed with neck pain occurring if I turned over onto the wrong side. It's funny how you can be grateful for discomfort. As I thought about my prior pains, I was indeed thankful for having only a stiff neck and a stone mattress.

I could see the Yongxing monastery crawling up the side of Beishan Mountain from my hotel window. I wanted to go there. *Too far to walk*, I thought, *but how I would get there was a mystery to me.* I had no GPS, and the sum total of my Chinese Mandarin vocabulary was limited to *xiè xiè* (thank you) and *nǐ hǎo* (hello). I had to find someone who could help me navigate the city. I decided to try my luck with Wu, the twenty-something desk clerk who had tried so hard to communicate when I arrived.

I stopped on the third floor and peeked into the dining room, where the breakfast buffet was set up—this wasn't a Days Inn, and I wasn't in Kansas. The only food items I recognized were boiled eggs and rice porridge. I discreetly put a few eggs in my backpack, retreated politely from the room, and headed to the lobby.

Round-faced and smiling behind the front desk, Wu greeted me with a fully translated, printed version of my son-in-law's late-night email, listing the ten top things to do in Xining. Wu had underlined the names of the places so that cabbies and bus drivers could easily understand where I wanted to go. It was my personal Rosetta stone. I pointed to the monastery and, using his cell phone translator, Wu said, "Bus. Bus 21 or 98." "Will it bring me back?" I asked his phone. It didn't answer, but Wu did. "No." *Maybe I would save the monastery until the next day, when I hoped to be better oriented to my new surroundings.* However, I did learn that there was an easy bus to the city center, the art museum, and the cultural museum. Apparently, it was also an easy walk, but that part got lost in translation. Because I suffer from acquired topographical disorientation, or directional dyslexia—I'm always getting lost—a bus was a better option.

I left the lobby, went outside, and was at a complete loss as to how to find the correct bus stop. Forlorn and frustrated, I pivoted, pushed through the large doors to go back inside, and went up to the front desk. Wu left his position and escorted me to the door, pointing in the direction of across the street and to the right. The Chinese, like the Mongolians, had no concept of pedestrian crossings, so simply getting to the bus stop took an act of courage.

It turns out that for one yuan (50 cents), you can ride any one of the dozens of shiny new buses that run up and down the broad flower-lined avenues to practically anywhere. Once I arrived somewhere, people were happy to tell me to get off the bus and where to catch the next one, if necessary.

Suffice to say, I had a fabulous day visiting the Qinghai provincial museum (fifty percent current affairs and history, fifty percent propaganda) and the art museum, with only a single gallery of contemporary Chinese art. Both museums shared a large, shady park and plaza that were full of people doing tai chi, a man playing a soulful tune on a flute (albeit in competition with Chinese national music blaring from loudspeakers), children flying kites, and a seller of Tibetan-style yogurt. I was offered a taste of the yogurt but declined to purchase some, in a foolish attempt to protect what was left of my digestive harmony. I listened to the strains of the flute and marveled at a sign explaining socialism in a way that any democrat would be proud to support. After some minutes of contemplation, I left the park to find my way to the grand Dongguan Mosque, the largest in the province, dating back to 1380 AD.

The preferred hijab is a black velvet scarf. Muslim men wear the familiar little white skull caps. It wasn't too hard to find the right bus to the mosque; I simply asked people wearing a hijab or a skull cap. When I boarded the bus, a little girl wearing a red neckerchief with her school uniform gave me her seat and then practiced a little English—something that happened often while I was in Xining.

Museums are nice experiences; trying the local food and shopping are fun. But this journey was all about the people that I met along the way, especially those who helped me order lunch or find my way back to my hotel, even when I was actually just two blocks away but helplessly lost. The highlight of my day was grabbing the arm of an elderly gentleman who was walking with a cane and struggling to use a cross walk—a dangerous endeavor even for a sprightly person—on a busy street. At first the old man looked like he might hit me with his cane, but then he relented and allowed me to walk with him. On the other side of the street, he nodded his head, said *xiè xiè,* and went on his way. *Of course, as you may have guessed, I might not have gotten across that street without him!*

I decided to have dinner at a Muslim mutton kabob shop that serves *dong dang ma xuewa*—hand-clasping mutton. It was only twenty yards away from where I stood, lessening the chance of getting lost. There were several young men but only one girl working harder than anyone else, and the only one who would take my order—three kabobs and a slice of grilled spicy round bread. I noticed a table with four chairs where a smiling family of three was sitting. I grinned, pointed at the empty seat, and then pointed at me. In response, they motioned for me to join them.

The boy, about eight years old, could speak a bit of English with prodding from his parents, and both of them understood a little. The mother was a nurse, the father a policeman. By the end of the meal, we were all sharing their dinner, and they refused to let me pay the nine yuan (about four dollars) for my order. Luckily, I had a pretty homemade key chain in my backpack for the mom and a Marvel miniature to give the boy.

I decided to walk while it was still light, hoping that I had made a mental inventory of good landmarks. The side streets, full of a variety of small shops (some fairly dicey looking, especially the cigarette and booze stores), gave off a distinct fragrance of cigarettes, auto fumes, and sewage—a bouquet of smells reminding me that this shiny new city was built on old land and infrastructure. On the bigger streets, what was left of ancient Chinese walls camouflaged giant cranes that were being used to build new monuments to progress.

The next morning, I caught a cab to the Yongxing monastery, the one I had seen from my bedroom window. The ride didn't take long, but I was too busy looking at people and storefronts, architecture, and back window vistas, to really pay attention to the route. I remember that the cab turned into a long narrow road to the entrance to the temples, which stretched up the mountainside to its very top. A few people wandered around the lower temples and gardens.

A monk, sitting and eating an apple, barred my entrance into the large sanctuary on the first level; so I strolled through the bonsai garden and then started up the stone stairs to the next level. Before I had climbed the second step, the monk tapped me on the shoulder . . . and handed me an apple. He sauntered down a different path, and I continued up. The temple on that level was closed, so I tried to decide whether to continue climbing or return to the bottom of the mountain to try to figure out my way back to the hotel.

It was then that I spied a small man, dressed all in the blue—the uniform of the people who serve the monks and take care of the shrines and grounds. He beckoned me over, but as I followed him, compelled by my curiosity, he disappeared up the next flight of stairs. I climbed after him but didn't see him at the top. Since I had entered the back of the sanctuary, I rolled the prayers wheels lining the outer walls while I made my way to the front. He wasn't there . . . and then he was. Again, he gestured for me to follow him, and again he disappeared up the steps. I climbed up five more levels, finding him and then losing sight of him, until I finally saw him waiting in front of an open temple. He summoned me inside.

"I don't know how to pray in a Vajrayana style. I learned Theravada Buddhism in Cambodia." The words tumbled out of my mouth before I could even ascertain whether he understood English. A smile broke across his heavily lined face and, saying nothing, he took my hands and put them together in a sort of clasp; then he pushed them up to touch my forehead before placing them on my chest. He let go of my hands, clasped his own hands, and put them on his forehead, then his chest; then he knelt and placed his forehead on the floor, his clasped hands out in front of his head. I copied his movements, although it took me several times to get the sequence right.

As I got to my feet, the sensation that something strange had just happened washed over me. He was smiling and nodding his head in approval. I started to ask him who he was and why he had taught me how to pray; but before I could utter anything more than thanks, he was gone, and I was left to wonder.

I was light-headed and a little dizzy as I found my way back down to the monastery entrance and walked past the fortune tellers and souvenir sellers out through the front gates to the narrow road that my morning cab had taken. I was in an old industrial area, rusty and unwelcoming. I quickened my pace and walked until I got to a large street, heavy with traffic. If only I had a better sense of direction and geography, I would have realized that I was a mile at most from my hotel. *If only.* I showed a passerby my hotel card and, true to the angels of Xining, he pointed to a bench across the road and said "98."

During the next couple of days, strangers took my photo and worried if it wasn't perfect; people on the streets returned my smiles and *nǐ hǎo(s),* first with suspicious glances and then with big grins. A young woman, seventeen-year-old Jong Wen Qing, whom I met while trying to find a dumpling and noodle shop, treated me to a bowl of very spicy mutton-stuffed dumpling soup, chicken feet, and duck neck bones. She insisted on paying, and I insisted that she take the neck bones and feet home with her.

I saw Qing several times after our first encounter. One evening we walked to a large central plaza and watched a nightly ritual in which dozens of Tibetans danced to boom boxes playing Tibetan music. We wandered over to a snack street, an old street about four city blocks long, crowded with tiny shops that were cooking all manner of seafood and other finger foods of unidentified origin. Throngs of people walked along eating, chatting, listening to hawkers, and eventually shopping at some of the merchandise stalls at the end of the road. From there we visited her family home—a small, cluttered apartment on the fifth floor of a walk-up. Her mom brought out plates of fruit that looked like they came from the day-old bargain bin, and her younger brother and sister plied me with questions about America.

On my last full day in Xining, the desk clerk, Wu—either afraid that I would get lost or mugged by an underground driver who gave me a ride, or because he had never been there and had caught the tourist bug from me—offered to take me to the Ta'er monastery when his shift ended. By ten o'clock, we were on a city bus. Arriving at our destination, Wu sat me down on a stone wall with a lovely view of the Nanchan Han Buddhist temple, which was perched on an overlook high above, while he went off in search of a private car willing to give us a *paid* lift to the Ta'er monastery. In less than ten minutes, Wu was back and beckoned me over to a small car. We had a ride, along with another couple whose truck was on the fritz. The pregnant lady, Wu, and I cozied up in the backseat; her husband sat up front with the driver, and we were off to the Ta'er temple, which was less than fifteen miles away from Xining in an area heavily populated by Tibetans (although most of the tourist throngs were Han Chinese with a sprinkling of Europeans). The temple had been built in 1577 in memory of Tsong Khapa, the founder of a branch of Tibetan Buddhism called the Yellow Hat Sect. It was also a *gompa,* an ecclesiastical university. A sacred place, it combined both Han and Tibetan styles of architecture on the mountain slopes. It was immense, and so were the crowds. People came from all over China to see dozens of large sculpted Buddhist deities made from yak butter and wander through one magnificent shrine on the way to gawk at and appreciate another.

After I beseeched them for a drink, a group of students gave me a bottle of water because I had none, and no way to get any. They adopted me, eager to speak English and show off their country's cultural treasures. For his part, Wu was happy to let them take charge for a while, which allowed him to rest from his challenging tour guide duties. On the bus back to the hotel Wu slept, his large round head on my shoulder. He had worked the night shift and, his good deed done, dozed all the way to town.

On my final morning in Xining, Wu took me out for a goodbye breakfast of beef noodles, a Qinghai specialty of northern cuisine. When we finished eating, he signaled a cab and sent me off to the airport that sent me on my way to the land of giant pandas, Chengdu. ∎

Post Script: As I tried to make sense of my epiphany at Yongxing monastery, I had to go back to my beginning. Born in the height of World War II of an eastern European orthodox father and the descendant of generations of Jewish grandmothers, I was keenly aware that I was Jewish. Both the holocaust and the marginalization of Jewish tradition in Chicago public schools (where we celebrated Christmas holidays and made no mention of Hanukkah or the Jewish high holy days), I knew early on that to deny my heritage was an existential threat to Jews. On the other hand, Jewish orthodoxy, like any other Judeo-Christian orthodoxy, and by derivation—Islam, firmly places women in a subordinate role. Even as a youngster, I knew that I would never be an observant Jew, but not an atheist. What I do believe in is a universal life force, a spirit that runs through the cosmos.

Occasionally, I have been swept up in the current and have come face-to-face with a sense of the divine. They occur anywhere. It happened while daydreaming on a sun-drenched boulder above Lake Jenny in the Grand Tetons, and then again standing on the bema in a Jewish Temple surrounded by the ghosts of five generations of Jewish mothers while we named my granddaughter for my favorite aunt. I felt it when an impoverished old woman placed her most precious possession, an ancient wooden Buddha in my hand to protect me from tigers and malaria. Another powerful connection came in a primeval garden outside of Estefan Iran. Standing in that garden I knew down to my cells that I was standing on ancestral ground—that my ancestors walked that ground. If an experience wasn't quite divine it was certainly one of a deep connection to my humanity. I had one of such epiphany at Yongxing monastery.

CHAPTER PHOTO CREDIT: Making friends outside the Taer Monestary, Juban Old Alley, Huangzhong, Xining, Qinghai Province, China. *The Carole J. Garrison Family Archive.*

Hanging with a group of "wanabe English speakers" in Taer Monestary. *The Carole J. Garrison Family Archive.*

Finding a fashion ally. *The Carole J. Garrison Family Archive.*

Admiring a Thangka artist at work. *The Carole J. Garrison Family Archive.*

Learning to pray Tibetan Buddhist style. *The Carole J. Garrison Family Archive.*

Early morning Tai chi in the park. *The Carole J. Garrison Family Archive.*

Keeping Tibetan dance and music alive. *The Carole J. Garrison Family Archive.*

Dongguan Mosque in the heart of Xining. *The Carole J. Garrison Family Archive.*

Inside the Northern Buddhist Temple high up on Tulou Mountain. *The Carole J. Garrison Family Archive.*

Having a good-bye breakfast with Mr. Wu from the hotel. *The Carole J. Garrison Family Archive.*

Mr. Wu and I at Taer Monestary. *The Carole J. Garrison Family Archive.*

10 Chengdu, China

The ticket counter girl in Xining did not recognize the fact that the airline had neglected to put a space between "Ms." and "Carole," so she thought the name on the ticket was incorrect until a supervisor approved it. After suffering anxiety over the validity of my ticket, I had to do something really strange. I had to fill out an airport release and discharge form that included my age, health status, and blood pressure. However, as you would expect, there was nowhere to have my blood pressure taken. The airline's agent finally relented and wrote something in the box that satisfied its process.

Relieved, I noticed for the first time that four-foot tall robots were gliding through the airport, delivering messages and announcing passenger instructions, even in the passport control area. The flight down to Chengdu was run-of-the-mill, but what I learned in that airport was *auspicious* (a favorite adjective the Chinese use to describe something positive and

fortunate). Most airport restrooms in China have Asian toilets, which are difficult to use without peeing on yourself and even harder to stand up from afterwards. But, as I happened to discover, the stalls designated for the handicapped in the Chengdu airport all have Western-style toilets.

I had booked a room in a small hotel online and, although I had no guarantee that it would be accustomed to foreign tourists, the description seemed pretty nice. Still, I wasn't sure what to expect from the Chinese booking agency I had used; after my recent experience in Xining, I was apprehensive. On the way to the hotel from the airport, when I saw the signpost for an alley (alley was the only part of the name I could understand), I offered a silent prayer that the cab driver wouldn't turn there. Nevertheless, he did; then he stopped immediately, opened my door, and handed me my luggage.

The smell in the room was foul. My tongue swelled, and the noise was too loud even for earplugs to block out—especially since I had to open the window for air. It wasn't until morning that I realized my first-floor room overlooked three spicy Szechuan noodle shops and was located across the narrow road from two more. To make matters worse, it turned out that my little hotel was about twenty yards from the delivery entrance to the Kowloon mall, which is really a wholesale exhibition hall for clothes brought in from surrounding factories. It opened early and closed late—twelve floors of shops, with deliveries 24/7—all under my window. I learned that Sichuan pepper is really a citrus that numbs your tongue and mouth, just by inhaling it. (I had thought my arthritis was acting up in a strange way.) *The four-star Raffles hotel would have been a better choice than my no-star local accommodations.*

I took a pass on a spicy breakfast and opted instead for a big steamed bun. I had heard it was best to get to the Chengdu Research Base of Giant Panda Breeding—or simply the Chengdu Panda Base Camp—when it first opened so, gulping down my tasteless bun, I caught a cab and headed out to Panda heaven. My trip to Chengdu was all about the pandas. I could have flown in, taken a taxi to the camp and flown out in the evening, satisfying my purpose for stopping there. Happily, I didn't. The pandas were delightful, but so was the rest of Chengdu.

Despite a slight drizzle and the early hour of 8:00 a.m., there were long lines for admission and an even longer line snaking slowly around the fences that enclosed the pandas' outdoor playground and indoor baby panda nursery. The line moved slowly because everyone had a camera; although some had impressive photography equipment, most people had cell phones or pocket cameras. It didn't matter, since each cute panda behavior stopped the line and elicited an outcry of "oohs" and "ahhs," recognizable in any language. I was as enthralled with the bears as anyone. My heart pounded happily against my chest when mama panda gave in and hugged her annoying triplets after they woke her from a nap. When one of the oversized youngsters climbed a tree and began to chomp on a bamboo stick, I sighed with pleasure right along with the hundreds of others who were clustered around the viewing fence.

I strolled through panda art galleries and history displays—pandas have been around for some eight million years—and drank hot chocolate at one of the panda cafés. I avoided the plethora of kiosks selling souvenirs, which I bought much cheaper at a grocery store around the corner from the hotel. I went to Chengdu for the pandas, and I wasn't disappointed.

By the time I returned from the Panda Base Camp, I had been given a new room on the fifth floor, on the other side of the building, with working air conditioning. *Life was good*. I was even able to get some laundry done, although a clerk had told me there was no laundry service. So I asked a different clerk, who said he could send my laundry out for me. The rule for foreign travelers: keep asking the same question in different ways until you get the information you need. This was quite a challenge.

While visiting the Manjushri monastery (Song Dynasty, 960-1279 AD) on my own, I found my way to Jinli Street, which dates back to the Qin Dynasty (221-206 BC). Now restored, the street was something like an Asian flea market, where I could bargain for worn and slightly faded old shadow puppets as well as several small faux resin Buddha charms. The man selling the charms was more than happy to sell me all I wanted. The female antique seller, however, was reluctant to give up the pair of fifteen-inch puppets, a man and woman dressed like courtiers from an ancient Chinese empire. She kept gesturing toward a newer set. Eventually, a young man who spoke English came to my assistance and convinced her that she would only make a sale if she parted with the older twosome. A ploy to raise the price? I didn't think so. But then I was so delighted with my treasure that I probably didn't pay attention to how much the yuan I gave her converted into dollars. At a more upscale shop, I purchased a Chinese chop, a traditional stone carving engraved with my name on the bottom to use as an artist stamp. I tried Chengdu's famous dish at a tiny rustic restaurant, tucked in between older buildings that lined the street. The Szechuan tofu nearly caused a relapse of my swollen tongue.

There were only thirty-four acres of authentic old China left in Chengdu at the time of my visit; however, a poor China remains in the alleys and side streets. I saw some of the city on my own but, in a delightful turn of events, two college students escorted me to the rest of Chengdu's highlights. Little Zang, the son of Mr. Zang, an accountant I had met by chance while eating lunch at a noodle shop in Xining, came to the hotel (on the orders of his father) to entertain me for a day.

Little Zang and his friend arrived bearing a deluxe box of moon cakes and cookies. Both boys were sweet and young. Little Zang was a pharmacy major, loved Disney movies (including *Frozen*, which I detested), and art. His friend was an automation engineer. We set off to visit, and in some cases revisit, Chengdu's famed museums and gardens. The lushly landscaped gardens—like those in Du Fu's Thatched Cottage Park—and the temples of Chengdu were as visually different from the wild, empty expanse of Mongolia's grass steppes as white is from black, yet both offered a spiritual serenity that filled my soul with harmony and peace. Whether I walked the garden paths alone or with Little Zang and his buddy, I was transported to centuries past and the glory that was Chinese civilization.

Because I am an avid film buff of Chinese historical dramas and legends, a trip to a museum that celebrated the characters from the internationally celebrated movie *Red Cliff,* which reenacted the great battle of Chibi (AD 208), was like walking among familiar old friends. Little Zang was amazed that I knew each character as well as any Chinese person would. I sipped rare Chinese teas and let myself be talked into purchasing a tin of buckwheat tea, but I declined to buy more expensive items in the gift shops and artisan stalls. I admired the pagodas and temple pavilions, snapped covert photos of monks and worshippers, and asked strangers to take photos of me in front of the lush foliage and graceful ancient gates.

Little Zang, instructed by his father to take me only to the best restaurants, was chagrined when we wound up at a sidewalk table eating take-out food. On the other hand, he was more relieved than disappointed when I chose to return to my hotel to rest and cook a bowl of Ramen noodles, rather than to visit Chengdu's very new snack and shopping street, and eat my dinner off a stick.

Riding through the streets of Chengdu, and watching traffic enter and exit the Kowloon Mall from the hotel lobby, I got the impression that China was one huge bee hive—with little worker bees, big bumble bees, queens, and drones. It was one enormous mass of undulating activity. But I was done being a tourist. I ate the bowl of Ramen noodles in my room and rested my tummy. I was flying early to Bhutan, via Kathmandu, and I wanted to be in good form. ∎

CHAPTER PHOTO CREDIT: Touring the Du Fu Thatched Cottage, a 24-acre park and museum in honour of the Tang dynasty poet Du Fu. *The Carole J. Garrison Family Archive.*

Enjoying the beauty of Tazishan Park. *The Carole J. Garrison Family Archive.*

Du Fu's Thatched Cottage. *The Carole J. Garrison Family Archive.*

Having my name carved into a soapstone chop. *The Carole J. Garrison Family Archive.*

Admiring the bonsai at Baihuatan Park. *The Carole J. Garrison Family Archive.*

Enjoying the tranquility and beauty of Wenshu temple. *The Carole J. Garrison Family Archive.*

Momma and toddler panda at the Chengdu Panda Breeding Research Center and Dujiangyan Breeding Yefang Research Center. *The Carole J. Garrison Family Archive.*

11 Bhutan

I had hoped to see the Himalayas unfolding across the horizon, but the weather g-ds chose instead to envelop me in a cloud. Nevertheless, the day bestowed other joys in this authentic, gentle, and beautiful country.

Although I had spent less than twenty-four hours in Kathmandu (where I would soon return) in transit on my way to the Kingdom of Bhutan, it was obvious upon my arrival that the country shared none of Nepal's conspicuous characteristics.

Before I extoll the natural beauty and charming medieval culture of this tiny Buddhist kingdom at the top of the world, I think it's fair to say that discovering Bhutan's underbelly produced a greater sense of discontent than it would have had I not bought into the fantasy. Bhutan's gross happiness index is fueled in small part by its population's habit of chewing a mixture of areca nut and betel leaf. It's a tradition, custom, or ritual that dates back thousands of years in many

areas extending from Asia eastward and southward to the Pacific. The Bhutanese have always chewed it as a prophylactic against the cold and isolation of winter at eight thousand feet above sea level but today, young people chew it to mollify their desire for a more modern and freer society—the world they see on their smartphones. Adding to my disappointment as I tried to capture some of Bhutan's celebrated spiritual magic were the pockets of poverty, the influence of and exploitation by India, and the obvious challenges associated with trying to balance traditional cultural and environmental concerns with the growing stress placed on local land use, native plants, animals, and ecosystems along with a larger carbon footprint due to tourism.

My guide, Tashi, was short and squat with a round face and a pleasant disposition. Our driver was taller and thickset, quiet and polite. They wore high socks that barely came up to the hems of their traditional cover—a knee-length woven jacket, belted at the waist (and looking for all the world like a bathrobe). We started off in Paro, the location of Bhutan's only international airport, but quickly headed out of town to Thimphu, the capital and largest city. Tashi chatted amicably and provided information about his small country. He claimed that a million years ago, the Bhutanese descended from a giant monkey. *Works for me, given Darwin's theories of evolution.*

According to Tashi, this little country of 800,000 people, sitting above the clouds, was struggling to preserve its soul and environment. Its last snowfall was in 2016, suggesting the effects of climate change, and the increase in unusually heavy monsoon rains threatens to rupture lakes and bring whole villages down the mountainsides. The Bhutanese don't build structures taller than six stories high, the height of the king's palace. Although shorter buildings might be built out of deference to the monarchy, my guess is that a country sitting on a seismic mountain range doesn't have the wherewithal to build skyscrapers that can withstand frequent earthquakes. So it doesn't.

Actually, I experienced an earthquake while I was visiting an eleventh-century monastery and fort. The jolt was so intense and over so quickly that I hardly registered what was happening. I was standing barefoot in the inner courtyard—in a structure made of wood and stone. I felt the shock, stared saucer-eyed at Tashi and, in the next second, was almost run over by a small herd of crimson-robed novice monks who tumbled out of their second-story rooms and fled down into the courtyard, out the main doors, and down the stairs to the open yard below. "Earthquake?" I asked. Tashi and a temple guard confirmed that it was indeed an earthquake. Then Tashi grabbed my hand and hurried me down the main staircase and out onto the lawn. I considered leaving the grounds because aftershocks can be dangerous, but the monks sounded the all clear before I could escape. Nervous giggles accompanied them as they filed back into the courtyard, with us trailing closely behind.

Tashi and I shed our shoes again and entered the main sanctuary to view the paintings that depict the ascension to ultimate enlightenment of the Buddha.

We were halfway around the sanctuary when dozens of monks entered the temple, sat down in long rows, and began chanting. I assumed the chant was a response to the earthquake, but it was actually a memorial service— something like a Catholic mass, Buddhist style. We were invited to stay and directed to sit with the bereaved family on cushions lining the walls. Then monks served us Tibetan milk tea and handfuls of rice roasted in honey and sugar. My eyes glistened with tears, so moved was I by the experience of listening to the chanting of the monks and their sacred music. It felt like we had been invited to stay since we all had experienced the earthquake together, but I had no one to ask if this was true. Tashi and I had stopped at this monastic fort on a whim, as well as for a chance to roll another sacred Mani prayer wheel for my colleague, Victor. Instead, I survived a seismic jolt and found myself a participant in a sacred ritual, rather than just a casual onlooker.

But I digress. My four days in Bhutan were packed with heart-stopping drives up narrow, winding mountain roads to visit monastic forts and memorial stupas—Buddhist monuments used for enshrining sacred relics that overlook lush valleys and emerald green terraces of rice. The towns offer unique shops, Thangka painters, penis carvers (penises are a big part of Bhutanese creation mythology), weavers, and fabulous textiles. The Bhutanese, like the Chinese, sell their version of Cordyceps, named *Yartsa gunbu*, which is a combination of moth larva (caterpillar) and a parasitic fungus. The high-priced "worms," as the infected larvae are called, are believed to cure everything from hair loss to hepatitis. Too pricey for my blood . . . but I did buy several pieces of old textiles. (Most will probably end up in more lap quilts on Beatrice's couch, but I couldn't resist.) In the mountains, trees were replaced with ghost forests—tall poles with narrow white or colored flags planted in memoriam. Closer to the ground were clusters of TsaTsas; these curious, small cylindrical cone-shaped objects on stupas, under overhangs of rock and alongside many roadways, are also made to commemorate the dead.

Tashi took photos of me with older women at the memorial stupa who were praying for the well-being of family members in the nearby hospital, with a lovely elderly man at the monastery of compassion where families bring ailing babies to be healed, and of school kids in their traditional uniforms. I knew that Victor was going into surgery. *It was all hands on deck.* So when Tashi took a photo of me with anyone rolling a prayer wheel (usually an older observant Buddhist), I used the occasion to solicit him or her to add Victor to their prayers.

In temples, I learned the story of the four friends: elephant, monkey, rabbit, and bird—the essence of communal harmony and the heart of Bhutanese philosophy. In this story of four unlikely friends who together plant and harvest a crop, each contributing its own special talent to get the job done, the bird is the hero, not the elephant. Size and strength are not supreme. I saw the images of the four harmonious animals on postcards, in art galleries, and even woven into wall hangings.

And finally, the *pièce de résistance* of Bhutan. We attempted to make the four-mile round trip mountain trek up to the Tiger's Nest, the fifteenth century monastery perched 10,232 feet above sea level. The steep trail that hugs the side of the mountain has a small café at its midpoint. Many tourists ride ponies up this first leg of the journey but, for me, riding a pony would have been worse than walking. There were times I thought my lungs would burst. Knee pads, walking sticks, expensive New Zealand trekking boots, and a very patient guide only got me as far as the café. By the time we made it there, I was spent, although other hikers marveled at my stamina. Standing at the midpoint, looking toward Tiger's Nest at the top of the mountain, I knew that there was a whole range of different peaks still in front of me. The real climb had only just begun. I decided to go back downhill and save my energy for the next challenge, perhaps one of more consequence.

As I left Bhutan to return to Nepal, this time with an unobstructed view of the Himalayas' tips above the clouds, I realized that the pandas had been a side trip. In fact, all of Europe was a side trip to my journey. Bhutan held some disappointments, but none that diminished the sense of empowerment and spirituality that infused my very being while I was there. I had no interest in simply wandering through the labyrinth of life, being herded by the walls of social expectations. I was on the maze wall, and I was beginning to see the heart that connects all paths. ■

CHAPTER PHOTO CREDIT: Paying homage at the tomb of Bhutan's late king, Bhumibol Adulyadej. *The Carole J. Garrison Family Archive.*

Outside the Chime LHakhang temple where people bring their children for healing. *The Carole J. Garrison Family Archive.*

One of the ladies I convinced to roll the prayer wheels for my friend Vic's recovery. *The Carole J. Garrison Family Archive.*

Hiking in the rice fields of Paro. *The Carole J. Garrison Family Archive.*

Having a group hug with local school boys in their school uniforms. *The Carole J. Garrison Family Archive.*

Halfway up to Tiger's Nest monastery that hangs far up on a cliff overlooking the Paro valley. It is one of the "tiger lairs" where the Buddhist master Padmasambhava, also known as Guru Rinpoche, is said to have meditated in the eighth century. *The Carole J. Garrison Family Archive.*

12 Nepal

Nepal was the centerpiece of my first round-the-world trip more than thirty years ago. From the moment I watched the silly Eddie Murphy movie, *Golden Child*, all I wanted to do was visit Kathmandu to hear the monks chanting and the sounds of the *dung-chen,* the long horn. Since that time I have become more educated about Tibetan Buddhism. What I love most is the meditation music of a Tibetan monastery with singing bowls, wind chimes, gongs and Buddhist monks chanting and praying.

I knew nothing more about the city than what I had seen in the movie and could glean from hippie travel sites. I was so protective of my escapade that I made my mother wait for me in New Delhi while I went on to Calcutta (where I got food poisoning), and from there to Kathmandu. A woman traveling alone in 1987 was rare, and a sick woman alone was even rarer. I won't retell that journey, save to say that, despite vomiting

from what felt like every orifice to being watched by the king's secret police, my first trip to Nepal was magical. It was then that I met Sonam, a young woman working in a Tibetan carpet factory and living in the adjacent Tibetan refugee camp, who would become one of my dearest friends.

Over the years I often returned to Nepal, sometimes for my birthday, which I celebrated with Sonam and her family on their rooftop sharing *momos*— spicy stuffed Tibetan dumplings— and salty yak tea. In 2008 I assisted Sonam, her husband, and their three daughters to immigrate to Canada. By the time I planned this latest trip, only Sonam's elderly parents, her oldest sister, Chonyi, and a younger sister, Yangpa and her family remained in the refugee camp. It was they I planned to visit on a convenient side trip from my main itinerary. Because they had barely survived a devastating earthquake in 2015, and according to Sonam not yet recovered, I wanted to visit and see if I could be of help.

Sonam called within weeks of my departure from the States. Yangpa's seven-year-old son had been identified as a reincarnated Tulka Lama, and the family was taking him to India to live with the Dali Lama. The entire family would not be in Nepal when I arrived, although they might return toward the end of my stay. I would spend nine days in the country with no place to go. I was not happy. Kathmandu was no longer a new adventure. I didn't want to trek; I didn't want to tour; I didn't want to find a hotel. I wanted to visit with the family and live in the camp. I wanted to do something different, so I decided to take a side trip from my side trip. I emailed Yangpa: "Do you think I can get a visa and a tour to Bhutan?" Yangpa hooked me up with a neighbor who worked for a regional travel agency, and Bhutan became my new destination. If the family was still gone when I returned to Kathmandu, I would figure something out.

I arrived in Nepal the evening before my departure to Bhutan and stayed at a small guest house owned by the Boudha monastery. Nepal was dirtier, poorer, and less appealing than I remembered it. The night was rough, and a cold shower didn't help. Between the barking feral dogs and a clanging street band, followed by dancers in wild mop-like headdresses who were celebrating a Hindu holiday by parading under my window, there was no rest. It was rainy and the streets, mostly unpaved and muddy, were crowded with monks and ordinary people—both Buddhist and Hindu. Dominating the skyline was the Boudha stupa. Many people, some in Western clothes but many more in traditional Tibetan garb, headed in the direction of the stupa to roll prayer wheels and make their circum-ambulations. I found a dingy restaurant for a beer and a plate of momos.

Yangpa and her family were back in Kathmandu by the time I returned from Bhutan. Yangpa's brother, a monk at the Boudha monastery, had delivered my larger suitcase in my absence, and the family was awaiting my arrival. I had a tiff with the cabbie, who didn't seem to know how to get to Jawalakhel, an area adjacent to the city. I helped him "understand" that he wouldn't be paid until I arrived at my destination so, after a few cellphone calls to Yangpa, he found his way. *It was at times like these that I was most grateful for the mobile phone revolution.*

In 2015, a series of severe earthquakes struck near the city of Kathmandu in central Nepal. The first earthquake on April 25 killed 9,000 people with many thousands more were injured. More than 600,000 structures in Kathmandu and other nearby towns were either damaged or destroyed. The earthquake was felt throughout central and eastern Nepal, much of the Ganges River plain in northern India, and north-western Bangladesh, as well as in the southern parts of the Plateau of Tibet and western Bhutan. A series of aftershocks plagued the region, which has devastated rural villages and some of the most densely populated parts of the city of Kathmandu.

Four years later, the earthquakes destruction remains evident as I walk through the streets of Kathmandu. Most of the carpet factory lay in ruins, a mass of rubble where the weaving and coloring sheds once stood. The streets are filled with refuse and feral dogs. Nepalese Hindus, not Tibetans, ran the small stores that lined the dirt road to the cement houses that I used to consider picturesque and quaint. Now they just looked like hovels. So many Tibetans had left the camp and factory after the earthquake that poor Nepalese had moved into the unoccupied spaces, and neither they nor the remaining Tibetans had the resources to repair the damage or reconstruct the houses.

Chonyi met me at the top of the hill that led down to the family's two tiny bungalows, where Yangpa and Pema waited for me. Pema was dressed in a bright red costume because it was Children's Day in Nepal, and they wanted me to join them for the school performance. Within minutes, we were at the neighborhood elementary school, which was slated for closure at the end of term due to dwindling enrollment. The school was decorated; the children were noisy and happy. Pema, among the youngest students, was treated like a princess—no doubt in part because of her older brother's recent elevation in the Buddhist hierarchy, as well as her own indomitable personality. I was pleased to note that, even while she danced, she clutched the panda bag I had brought her from Chengdu.

My days passed pleasantly enough—visiting Chonyi at what was left of the factory, sharing meals with the grandparents, and joining Yangpa and Pema at a local hotel pool for a swim one day. That day was a Nepalese-Indian holiday, so the streets were crowded with people wearing gorgeous, richly colored silk saris and other splendid ethnic outfits. Nevertheless, the chaos, clutter, rubble, and dirt made everything unpleasant—including our pool outing.

During the days, I did not go to Kathmandu's infamous Freak Street, still frequented by older as well as younger backpackers, or even the local monasteries, choosing instead to hang with the family. Chonyi made momos and dal, which we ate sitting on the floor in the combination living room-sleeping room. But nights were another story. I slept on a mattress in a small alcove, with a curtain for my door and a hot water thermos by my bed so I could make coffee in the morning. The family's bathroom was outside, and locked. There were no lights, except for a flashlight and, if I went out the door, the noise from turning all the locks woke up everyone. The toilet was broken; the shower was a pail of heated water from the kitchen and cold water from the tap. All the fixtures were grimy, and the clean towels were threadbare. Strange dogs patrolled the area. I had tolerated the moldy showers and hard beds in China, but I was not prepared for this. I had gotten *soft* or *old* . . . or both. Certainly, I had endured much worse in the Cambodian countryside in the early 1990s and, surely, I had used the same toilet on my earlier visits. Despite how much I adored this family, I was ready to leave. But first I should explain why my *no shopping* pledge required the assistance of Yangpa before my departure.

My bulging suitcase was only thirty-one inches tall, and the shocking pink carry-on was the size of a medium gym bag. I couldn't take anything heavier on this trip for fear that I would throw out my back. On the occasions that this had happened, my life had become a haze of disability—I still had enough residual arthritis pain that I needed to avoid incurring any more. No space in my luggage meant no shopping. *No shopping. Ha!* By the time I reached Nepal my carry-on, which had emptied out in Europe, was again bursting at the seams with *no shopping* items. I no longer needed my jacket or top-of-the-line hiking boots. I needed to divest myself of the extra pieces of gear and the few purchases I had made.

The boots and jacket were no-brainers because I was headed to the equator. However, I was surprised by the amount of *no shopping* I had managed to accumulate. There was a ceramic pomegranate from Turkey along with several small, painted bone box miniatures, beaded string bracelets, and a pair of silver braided earrings. I guess I had thought that anything smaller than a Turkish rug didn't count. From Russia there was a black lacquer box painted with a scene from the fairy tale, "Prince Ivan, the Firebird, and the Gray Wolf," and two small *matryoshka* nesting dolls— one a chicken, the other a cat. I also had a handful of gallery brochures of paintings by a Russian-Buryatia artist whose works cost up to hundreds of thousands of dollars. In Mongolia, the art was not only more affordable; the original art I loved was small enough to fit in an eighteen-inch plastic tube: small paintings of wild horses and shamanistic figures, and one rural scene painted on sheep's leather.

A quick trip to a tourist shop before Beatrice arrived had resulted in a couple of pairs of cashmere gloves and a few felted sets of finger puppets. *Everything seemed extremely small so as not to be a problem.* Two yak leather wallets and two passport holders completed my Mongolian acquisitions. China was more tempting, and it was difficult to restrain myself. Stuffed into my bag was a pair of embroidered green and red canvas shoes purchased at the huge wholesale fashion mall, three small paintings of aspects of Tara, a female *bodhisattva* in Buddhist legend, and a pair of delicate antique Chinese shadow puppets. Of course,

I couldn't leave Chengdu without some panda souvenirs, and I didn't resist the temptation to buy several ink chops carved with my name and my granddaughters' names. Bhutan's legendary weavings proved to be the most irresistible. I found some pieces of large, older textiles and several small examples of various styles and designs representative of different ethnic weaving communities across the country.

Yangpa had a friend—of course she did. (Tibetans have a network of other Tibetans to assist them to survive in a country in which they have no official status.) The friend managed a small UPS store in Paton—a short but hair-raising bus ride away from the camp in Kathmandu traffic. We emptied out my shocking pink bag, put all my little gifts in a large canvas sack along with my hiking boots and a few other items, and delivered them to the UPS shop. Except the shop did not look anything like an official UPS franchise; rather, it appeared to be a small grocery and knick-knack store! Yangpa, sanguine about the reliability of her friend, insisted that my stuff would arrive in the States. By the time we returned to Yangpa's house, I no longer cared whether my treasures made it to their destination. I was not confident that I would ever see any of them again, and I had decided that the joy was in the discovery and not in the possession. I hoped I would still feel that way when I got home to West Virginia.

On the morning of my scheduled departure, Sonam's parents came to offer me a *khata*— a greeting scarf as a wish for happiness. They each put a long white khata around my neck, followed by Chonyi,

Yangpa, and Pema—until I was buried in scarves. Pema presented me with a small Mani wheel that I could carry with me. I was aglow from their kindness and welcoming gestures. Although I had brought nothing with me but inconvenience, still I was received and treated with as much hospitality as they could muster.

The weather g-ds had smiled on my way back to Kathmandu from Bhutan, but rather than giving me another gift, they sent Typhoon Mangkot to play havoc with flights to Taiwan. I had two choices: stay in Kathmandu until the weather cleared and the airports reopened, or give up my visit to Taiwan and fly directly to Cambodia. I chose Cambodia. I was exhausted from sleepless nights and spending the day in the inhospitable airport, fighting with China Southern Airlines and struggling with Wi-Fi that continually went out, leaving me with questions unanswered by my travel agents. Finally, confirmed on a flight to Phnom Penh, I waited a few more hours and then headed south, away from Mangkot and toward a hoped-for respite. ■

CHAPTER PHOTO CREDIT: Ignoring the dead dog on the street to the refugee camp. *The Carole J. Garrison Family Archive.*

Boudha Stupa dominates the skyline and Tibetan life. *The Carole J. Garrison Family Archive.*

The Jawalakhel Handicraft Center and Tibetan refugee camp. *The Carole J. Garrison Family Archive.*

Sharing a MOMO feast with Pima and her aunt. *The Carole J. Garrison Family Archive.*

Shopping along Freak Street. *The Carole J. Garrison Family Archive.*

Pima's class performing on Children's day. *The Carole J. Garrison Family Archive.*

Photo of the Dali Lama and Pima's brother, a newly identified Tukla Lama. *The Carole J. Garrison Family Archive.*

Pima and her uncle. *The Carole J. Garrison Family Archive.*

Rescued from no Wi-Fi by a feminist Indian merchant of Tibetan Thangka's. *The Carole J. Garrison Family Archive.*

Yangpa's mother and me. *The Carole J. Garrison Family Archive.*

13 Cambodia

Apparently, Kimsore thought I looked pretty feeble when I arrived in Phnom Penh—the result, I was sure, of twenty-four hours sitting in airports and riding on airplanes. But by the morning, with the exception of a mild case of dysentery, I was rested and relatively free of arthritis pain.

I stayed in Cambodia for almost a month, hanging out with my three g-dsons, their families, and other friends—people who had worked for me in Cambodia in the 1990s, and over the years had become extended family. I've gone to Cambodia often to attend weddings, celebrate births, watch children grow up, offer motherly advice, and cheer them on. I omit the details of these visits from this account, preferring to include only those adventures that any wanderer to this country might experience, or those that continually amaze me, no matter how often I go to Cambodia.

In recent years, since his retirement, I've stayed with Kimsore—the eldest of my three United Nations interpreters, whom I refer to affectionately as g-dsons. He and his wife, Sopheap, live in a lovely Balinese-style villa, equipped with an air conditioner in one room on the main floor, which has been dedicated to me. *Lucky me.* It's a far cry from the lean-to that Kimsore occupied following Cambodia's civil war when he first came to work with me. It's also a home that is unique among the cement, fully air-conditioned, and sealed monstrosities that Cambodia's emerging middle and upper classes have built in the midst of the poor, who eke out livings as farm laborers or in the Chinese factories.

Kimsore delivered fresh coffee to my bedroom by six o'clock that first morning; then I had breakfast with Sopheap and their teenage son, Propei. By 10:00 a.m., Kimsore and I were on the way to Udong, the old capital of Cambodia (circa 1668), which is a forty-minute drive from Phnom Penh on the highway to Pailin. Kimsore and Sopheap had bought a lovely piece of land right across from a Buddhist meditation center at the foot of the mountain where ancient stupas, pagodas, and palaces dating back to the seventh century overlook the countryside. Small children, truanting from school, hawked flowers and incense. Monkeys climbed the parapets, unconcerned about the few tourists who were making their way to the top.

We climbed the mountain by the back road that runs past Kimsore's land. It was the same road that kings used when going to or coming out of a retreat.

The mountain, which by Bhutanese standards would be considered an anthill, was still a challenge of slippery steps and uneven rocky paths. In one of the old pagodas, there were murals of the story of Buddha's life, similar to those I had seen in the temples of China, Mongolia, and Bhutan. The paintings tell the same story, but here the characters look Siamese and wear traditional Siamese garb, whereas in northern Buddhist temples, they look either Indian or Tibetan and are dressed like early Hindu g-ds.

It was the end of monsoon season; the sky was gray, the air wet and cooler than Cambodia's usual temperature of ninety-plus degrees Fahrenheit. As I stood on a balcony of the former royal palace, I could see rich, verdant fields stretching out to the huge inland lake, the Tonlé Sap, which was full of floating villages and bulging at its banks from rainstorms of biblical proportions. (I once had provided civic education about the upcoming elections on one of these floating villages; as I talked, the people cleaned their little fishes.) Back at Kimsore's lot, we napped in hammocks strung across a small stand of trees, and then returned to his home in time for a dinner of rice, grilled pork ribs, and bitter soup.

A couple of days later, Kimsore drove me to Skon, the village where Beatrice and I had lived during the UN peacekeeping mission, called UNTAC, in 1992. Our traditional little wooden house had been torn down—gone was scoop tub bathhouse that our landlord had built for us and the outhouse in the back that I wouldn't use at night for fear of cobras, preferring instead a small red plastic bucket for nocturnal needs. The dilapidated villa next door was ruined. I remembered that the people who lived there had pigs that liked to wander into our front yard and chew the collars off my shirts while they hung out to dry. Kimsore omit who worked for me in Skon, took me to visit the aging mothers who had been our neighbors and whose children fetched ice for us, asked us to polish their nails, or came to sing Old McDonald Had a Farm for us in a funky mix of English and Khmer. We ate at the old restaurant across from the memorial to the Chinese and UN soldiers who had been killed in an attack by the Khmer Rouge during UNTAC. Although we feasted on traditional Khmer food, I declined to eat the barbecued jungle spiders, sautéed grubs, and steamed beetles.

After lunch we drove just outside the village to see my "chubby monk." He was the same monk who had been in charge of the village pagoda in the early 1990s, when I lived nearby. He had also performed the ceremony and blessing when I adopted my daughter, Tevi, in 1997. Every time I return to Cambodia, I make a pilgrimage to visit him. Our ritual repeats itself. We pray together, I give him a hundred-dollar bill as a donation, and he orders novice monks to shimmy up palm trees and cut down a branch laden with the best coconuts in the region. During this visit, the monk did a special chant to petition on behalf of Victor and his recovery.

Thervada Bhuddism, the majority religion of SE Asia, was the spiritual and social center of Cambodian life when I arrived in 1992. It was politically and socially prudent to show deference to the local monks and religious community, so we did. We used the villages' pagoda to organize civic education meetings and voter registration. We attended ceremonies with the local population and sought out the monks blessings at office openings, and celebrations. The nuns stopped at my house curious to see how I lived and to ask for western aspirin. They thought my PhD was the same as an MD and I could never persuade them otherwise—so I stopped trying. My chubby monk became my biggest fan, and I in turn developed a genuine fondness for him and a respect for his religious sincerity and role in the community. When I saw him this time, I wanted him to add his voice to those already beseeching the universe to heal my friend. That meant I had to be a genuine penitent in his tradition—a role I gladly assumed.

Before returning to Phnom Penh, Kimsore and I drove to Kampong Cham City, stopping to visit the Wat Nokor Bachey temple on the outskirts. The local people sometimes call the temple 'Wat Angkor,' since it was built in the era and style of Angkor Wat, the most famous temple in Cambodia. I prefer Wat Nokor because it's easier to get to and there are fewer tourists. A ticket to visit Angkor Wat costs $60 USD per day, whereas Wat Nokor costs only two or three dollars, and you get a little red string to protect your life force. Wearing the red string is a reminder that one must show compassion to all. I was still wearing one from the last time I visited, at least a year before. The pagoda women, elder women and nuns who weave the small red cotton strings, tied a new one on my left wrist. It made the one I wore look faded by comparison, but I decided that, if one was good, two were better.

Kimsore and I made one last stop before returning to Phnom Penh. We drove to a small village just south of Wat Nokor and near to the Mekong river to visit Nareth's elderly parents. The temperature hovered in the mid-nineties draining me of energy and covering my body in a sheen of sweat. Kimsore was immune to the heat but dragging as it was well past his daily naptime. We trudged up the steep wooden stair rungs to the second floor of the big wooden house. Nareth's parents stayed up there most of the time, too frail to go up and down. Their children who lived nearby brought food and Nareth had built a modern kitchen and bathroom up there—one they disdained to use if they could avoid it. They greeted me on the porch that lined the front of the house and offered fruit and water. But we could not be revived and within minutes we were all four stretched out on brightly colored woven mats for an afternoon siesta.

Sleep came quickly but my nap was short. As I lay between Kimsore and Nareth's mother I remembered the stories Nareth shared long ago. His father would teach him in a small curtained room inside the house. They would study by candlelight, careful that no light shone through to attract the attention of the Khmer Rouge. Had they been discovered, death would have come swiftly and brutally. This couple, nut brown from the sun and gnarled with age, had shepherded their children safely through civil war, Nixon's bombing campaign during the Vietnam war and finally through Pol Pot and the killing fields. How precious to be in their company. Good byes were bitter-sweet. I never knew if I would have the chance to see them again.

I heard the prayers before dawn. At first, I thought the occasion was a call to prayer from a nearby mosque, but it was the start of the Pchum Ben festival. This holiday lasts for two weeks, and its end traditionally signals the conclusion of the monsoon season. During this time, Cambodians get up very early in the mornings, cook rice and, using the palms of their hands, make sticky rice balls called *Bay Ben*. Before dawn, they take these Bay Ben, along with other offerings, to the pagoda. There, they participate in a ceremony to convene the "souls" of the deceased. At a certain point in the ceremony, the participants scatter the Bay Ben onto the ground or throw them deep into the woods, hoping to keep the ghosts at bay. Some people place rice balls for the *prett,* the damned, as well as the deceased who have no neighbors, friends, or families to commemorate them; they also honor those whose families cannot attend. *I find it interesting that this holiday occurs at the same time of year as Yom Kippur and All Saints Day, both holidays that focus on the dead . . . and that the Buddhist practice came first. As I recall, the chubby monk prayed for my father at my first Pchum Ben ceremony.*

I returned to the pagoda in Skon to celebrate the Pchum Ben festival with another of my g-dsons, Meng, and his large extended family. The chubby monk invited me to sit close to his dais, and I swear he winked at me during the chanting.

Another reoccurring event when in Phnom Penh is meeting with college students who are financially supported by a group of women in Ohio, Four Women for Women, which is dedicated to promoting women's education. When I'm in Cambodia, I act as the group's emissary to the students, providing them with information about the Ohio group as well as whatever encouragement I can. On this trip, I met with eighteen young women. The girls come from Pursat, Prey Veng, and Kampong Chinang provinces—all places that have benefited little from Phnom Penh's frenetic attempt to modernize.

As recently as eight years ago, young women like these had nothing to look forward to but a life of poverty and hardship; today, however, thanks to the Ohio group and others, they are bursting with optimism and planning to return to their communities, committed to building better lives for everyone. They are currently studying nursing, social work, community development, and accounting. *Although I did encourage them to think about becoming doctors, engineers, and bosses . . .*

No trip to Cambodia is complete without a stop at the farm and a day at the national art museum—two very different milieus, but both distinctly Khmer. Meng picked me up early one morning, and we drove seven hours in the opposite direction from Skon to his longan berry farm in Pailin, a northwestern province and former stronghold of the Khmer Rouge. The jungle that had covered Pailin and hidden its secrets had been cleared; the gemstones that had bought protection and military weapons had been depleted; and gone, too, were the ruthless Khmer Rouge guerrillas. Now there is only lush, virgin farmland. Meng owns three hundred and seventy acres. Although I own just ten percent of the acreage, he likes to tell people that it is *my* farm. We spent the morning installing solar light kits in the two shanties on the property so that the farm's tenants would have lights and could watch a small television.

Most of the locals live without running water or electricity. I walked, or I should say slogged, across the half of the farm that was swamped from monsoon rains, sweated like I was in a steam bath, and then passed out in a hammock until we feasted on a picnic lunch of chicken cooked with jackfruit, mango salad, and large, charcoal-grilled river fish. I had to throw away my shoes, but I loved being there with the farmhands, their children, and neighbors. The farm is planted with mangos, logon berries, corn, dragon fruit, and bamboo. Meng had found a natural spring, so the land is fully irrigated—even in the hot, dry season, which was coming soon. In areas with fewer crops, there were acres of green, green rice—a sight that always makes my heart leap with hope for a better tomorrow.

The long drive back to Phnom Penh allowed time to remember the boys, my translators, who I now affectionately consider my g-d sons. During the 1992 pre-election registration and civic education, they had become my eyes and ears. Moreover, they were my voice. Nareth understood the democratic principles supposedly reflected in this upcoming election. He thirsted for them; he struggled for them; he believed in them. He had the heart and soul of a patriot. Meng, on the other hand, was all business. He wanted a restored economy and opportunity. He was hungry to climb out of poverty and squalor. Meng also had hidden and run to escape the Khmer Rouge. For him, Untac wasn't the promise of some philosophical "good society." It was a means to a new economic beginning, a jumpstart into the twenty-first century and modernity. Meng was to Nareth as Forbes was to Mother Jones. The boys were at my beck and call. They were my shadows, my voice—my head and then as now—my heart. Kimsore joined our team later, a refugee from the camps who the UN recruited to help with the elections. Older than the boys he was quiet, solicitous and meek, belying his fortitude and compassion. He was just grateful to be alive and working. He and Nareth became like brothers and soon we became a foursome *to be reckoned with*.

"Momma," Meng called out to me as I stirred and sighed while remembering those days. "Are you okay?" he inquired. Roused from my temporary reminiscing, I turned to face him and smiling broadly I remember murmuring, "Oh, yes. I am quite okay and so happy to be with you."

The national art museum is also a place of hope. Over the years, the museum has prospered, undergone repairs, and regained priceless lost or stolen artifacts. (Many were recovered through political channels, others via legal challenges.) Hindu and Buddhist sacred sculptures, surrounded by beautiful foliage, crowd the galleries and are now organized with signage according to periods. (In 1992, it was a wreck of a building; sculpture, a lot of it broken, lay about helter-skelter.) Just behind the building is the newly reinstated college of fine arts, where youngsters, like Kimsore's son Propei, learn traditional dance and play ancient instruments. It has become a safe haven for Cambodian culture and a promise of its preservation for future generations.

Cambodia is full of centuries-old temples, predating Buddhism to the era when Hinduism was the region's religion and its temples were built to celebrate Hindu g-ds. Most temples have since been converted to represent Buddhism, but they retain the trappings of sacred Hindu architecture and culture. One of my favorites is Phnom Chisor. What I don't enjoy is the 461-step climb up uneven steps to reach the temple on top of the mountain. On this particular day, it was ninety-one degrees when I left Kimsore napping in a hammock at the outdoor food market and started climbing. Because the temple had been built in the eleventh century, it was worth the climb, but I had to keep assuring people along the way by saying *kyome aute slop* (I'm not dead) and *kadal nah* (very hot) but *aute panyaha* (no problem). There is also a pagoda and a small Buddhist monastery on top of the mountain. I remembered—too late—that the last time I had made this trek, I promised never to do it again.

Like most emerging economies in Asia, Cambodia is a country of contradictions. This fact was never more evident than when I accompanied another former employee to fetch his children from a top-end private international school, ironically abbreviated "CIA." Tuition ranges from $4,000 USD a year for kindergarten through sixth grade to $8,000 USD for grades seven through twelve. In the meantime, a typical annual salary in Cambodia is about $1,108 USD.

Arriving early, we went across the street to a Western-style coffee shop in a large modern development. The two-story condos were selling for one million dollars, and slightly smaller flats were going for $220,000 USD. A Walmart-size superstore was in the final stages of completion, as were other upscale boutique shops. However, not even a half-mile down the street was a neighborhood of shanties with tiny businesses spilling out onto rough, unpaved roads full of refuse, human and otherwise.

Another contradiction that startled me was the fact that Phnom Penh now boasts two high-end Japanese malls replete with gourmet Western and Eastern restaurants, indoor playgrounds, an aquarium, roller rinks, and state-of-the-art 4XD movie theaters. *West Virginia doesn't even have an IMAX.* I took several of my g-dsons' kids to the movies. I took Nareth and his sons, Purin and Norin to the movies. We saw *Small Foot,* an animated film. Although I would have preferred an adult action film, this was a first-time event for all of them, and *Small Foot* fit the bill.

After three weeks in Cambodia, life began to feel routine. I was *sabaye* (happy) but restless. I woke early, sometimes as early as 4:00 a.m., to Skype into a school board meeting that was taking place in the early evening in West Virginia. (I could attend meetings via Skype only when I had an internet connection. *Shocking, the level of participation technology has facilitated.*)

Sometimes the torrential rains or choruses of water-soaked frogs woke me early. Kimsore, who preferred lunch cooked at home by the housekeeper, had to nap each day after eating plenty of the food he enjoyed so much. On the other hand, he was reluctant to let me take a cyclo-cab or a tuk-tuk to the markets or museums on my own, so I rested a lot and became impatient. It was time to move on. I chose Luang Prabang, the ancient capital of Laos, as my next destination. ■

Postscript: My chubby monk passed away in 2019 of a stroke. He never had the opportunity to visit me in the States; a dream of his he often spoke about. The Trump administration refused his visa application.

CHAPTER PHOTO CREDIT: Visiting Garuda at the National Art Museum in Phnom Penh. *The Carole J. Garrison Family Archive.*

With my chubby monk in Skun. *The Carole J. Garrison Family Archive.*

Praying for Vic. *The Carole J. Garrison Family Archive.*

Ancient Stupa in Udong. *The Carole J. Garrison Family Archive.*

Climbing Udong Mountain to visit the former capital of Cambodia.
The Carole J. Garrison Family Archive.

Angkor period temple in Kampong Cham city. *The Carole J. Garrison Family Archive.*

Angkor period temple on the top of Chisor Mountain. *The Carole J. Garrison Family Archive.*

With Meng's family at Pchum Ben, a 15-day Cambodian religious festival, culminating in celebrations on the fifteenth day of the tenth month in the Khmer calendar. *The Carole J. Garrison Family Archive.*

Phnom Penh college students supported by Women for Women in Ohio. *The Carole J. Garrison Family Archive.*

Life along the Mekong River. *The Carole J. Garrison Family Archive.*

Buddha statutes everywhere. *The Carole J. Garrison Family Archive.*

With Nith, Norin and Purin at Nith's take out mango salad restaurant. *The Carole J. Garrison Family Archive.*

Grubs, spiders and crickets for sale in the Skon market. *The Carole J. Garrison Family Archive.*

Making a house-call to Naret's elderly parents in their village. *The Carole J. Garrison Family Archive.*

On the farm with my former UNTAC worker, Bun Leang. *The Carole J. Garrison Family Archive.*

Buddha statute at temple in Kampong Cham. *The Carole J. Garrison Family Archive.*

Buddha faces at Chi Sor mountain. *The Carole J. Garrison Family Archive.*

Greeting tourists at the bottom of Udong Mountain. *The Carole J. Garrison Family Archive.*

Alms begging in Skun; part of their daily life. *The Carole J. Garrison Family Archive.*

THE WANDERER

It was a relief to be in the small town of Luang Prabang, its charm and history protected by UNESCO, assuring that I would stay in the center of things. I arrived around 6:00 p.m. Even at that late hour the temperature on the airport thermometer was showing 95 degrees Fahrenheit. I caught a taxi into the town center with several other women. One unconventionally dressed, elderly woman who was apparently a frequent visitor to the area, pointed out an NGO called Big Brother Mouse, where one could volunteer to teach English. I made a mental note of the information but quickly forgot the location because I was preoccupied by scanning the streets for the name of my guest house.

We drove down a main street lined with small exotic local craft shops, coffee shops, backpacker guest houses, and restaurants. The taxi driver pointed out another street at the end of town; parallel to the Mekong, it was the night market where dozens of

sellers set up on the pavement between restaurants and stores. In the other direction, the street was book-marked by two enormous pagodas, which I planned to explore first thing in the morning. For the moment, however, my only desire was to like my accommodations—the ancient Luang Prabang hotel on Khunsour Road—find the nearest riverside restaurant, order a tall Lao beer and a sticky rice ball, and then go to bed!

I did like my guest house. It happened, however, to be owned and managed by Chinese, not Laotian, people—not an unusual situation. Although Luang Prabang's charm and architecture is protected, unfortunately UNESCO does nothing to shield the property rights of the locals.

Foreigners, mostly Chinese, are buying up all the houses and turning them into guest houses and restaurants, moving the Lao folk out into the 'burbs. This was the cause of considerable angst among the locals, not just in Laos but also in most parts of Southeast Asia that I visited. China was gobbling up real estate, mineral rights, and establishing all manner of factories and plants that took money out of the pockets of local people and put it into the coffers of Chinese capitalists and entrepreneurs. My conversations with locals often centered on their fears about China's aggressive economic infiltration.

Before I left Cambodia, I booked a Lao village tour. I had remembered taking one with my mother and brother years ago on my first visit to Laos and wanted to recapture the experience. However, somehow I missed the part where the tour company called it a leg-pumping trek and falsely assumed that I would be *Jeeped* to a village in Laos' rugged interior as we had been in the 1990s. This tour was an adventure for someone else, although I think that even a twenty-something trekker would have found it daunting. During the hike I worried most that I'd die from heat stroke or fall down and twist my ankle! That was if a snake didn't bite me in the jungle. (My guide, a small, compact young man in his mid-twenties named Lajly, told me that snakes often fall out of the trees, but he reassured me that they would either be dead or too hot to bite.)

Lajly and I started out on a short trip across the Nam Khan River in a long dugout canoe. By luck, we came upon a small herd of elephants and their mahouts, who were leisurely preparing to spend the day taking tourists to other hamlets and over the steep, rocky trails in and around the jungle and rubber plantations. Riding elephants wasn't an option on my tour, and neither was a special audience with a herd. I considered this a good omen for the rest of the day.

Not until I hiked to it did I realize that the Theung village of Lao Sung could only be reached by four hours of trekking on unshaded, rough dirt paths potholed from elephant tracks and dotted with large mounds of elephant poop. The temperature was close to one hundred degrees Fahrenheit, and the only shade came from the leaves of elephant ear plants—luckily, a plant quite abundant in Laos.

As Lajly was cutting leaves for us to carry like umbrellas, he related an old Lao fable. The story went that a merchant was traveling by elephant to

Southeast Asia. When they reached Laos, the elephant told his master that he was old and could not go any further. It was time for him to die. His master, who had great affection for the beast, buried him in the jungle, and the elephant ear plant grew from his ear. His eyes twinkling, Lajly said, "That's why so many elephant ear plants grow in Laos."

Occasionally, we would duck out of the sun by walking alongside the edge of a rubber plantation, or cool off by crossing a stream on a rickety footbridge made of twigs and vines. But mostly we walked in the unrelenting sun as it rose high above us in the sky. It was late morning by the time we reached the village; rather than exploring anything, I collapsed on a bench, closed my eyes, and didn't move for a very long time.

The village, with its bamboo huts and dirt yards, seemed intensely poor. The only inhabitants besides the goats and chickens were very young children—who appeared to spend their days unsupervised, running barefoot over the dirt—and very old women with gnarly hands and bright birdlike eyes that squinted from faces of wrinkled leather. We ate a simple homemade lunch prepared by an elderly couple whom I assumed were husband and wife. While we sat at a picnic table in front of a glorified shack, two little girls peeked out from the doorway to giggle and watch us; the apparent husband smoked on a homemade bamboo water pipe. Embarrassed by the poverty, I took off the necklace I was wearing, a colorful piece of costume jewelry, and presented it to our hostess. Although her toothless smile was shy, I think it was sincere.

Unfortunately, there was no shortcut back to the river, so we started walking down the sun-flooded trail at high noon. There was no Jeep service to call, no elephant to rescue me. Eventually, Lajly turned off the road, entering the jungle. "What are we doing? Are we there?" I asked, hoping we were close to the river. But no, Lajly was cutting through the jungle to get us out of the sun. I ignored the mosquitoes and did my best to keep hiking, even though I was unbearably hot. Lajly stopped and said, "This way; we have to climb down in order to reach the waterfall and the river." What way? All I saw was a black hole in the ground! "Climb down? Climb how?" I squealed as I looked into the dark abyss.

"It's okay," he replied, trying to reassure me. There's a ladder." I peered in closer. There was a rope ladder, the skinny wooden rungs about fifteen feet apart, descending further than the light. "I'll go down first," he said. "Then I can help you." What choice did I have? I could turn back to the sun-drenched trail, stay where I was and get bitten to death by mosquitoes, or go down the rope.

He directed my shaking foot down to each rung, while my hands clutched the cables with a death grip to slowly lower myself. At the base of the rope ladder, Lajly helped my feet touch solid ground and grinned at me. "Are we there?" I asked. "Close, close. It is just a little further," he answered. "Take my photo," I demanded with false bravado—my jeans were soaked with sweat. Close was still too far, but I was okay, and finally we arrived at the falls. Tourists were swimming in the cold pool or sitting on the deck drinking beer and wine. I lay down flat on a small deck off the base of the waterfall, trying to relieve my aching back. There was no relief, no euphoria—only dull shock. I fell asleep. When I woke fifteen minutes later, or maybe it was an hour, I was disoriented. When I tried to stand, my legs cramped from my hips to my toes. I was dehydrated.

Lajly gave me a bottle of water and assurances that the river and our boat were just a few paces away beyond the brush. *Next time, I will read the fine print*.

I woke early the following day, after passing out by eight o'clock the previous evening. It was late enough that I could hear noises coming from the small make-shift outdoor café across the road, but not nearly early enough to see the young monks leave their dormito-ries at the end of town to march to a starting point where they would disperse and begin their door-to-door begging for rice and alms. Disappointed to have missed the procession, I silently promised myself to awaken even earlier the next day. I made a cup of instant coffee and thought about my plans for that day, when I turned seventy-six—not a "Big O Birthday"—but, I thought, singular enough. I wanted it to be a special birthday . . . and special to someone other than me.

Phra Bounthong, a young monk I had befriended earlier in the week while visiting the two large pago-das I had passed on my arrival to Luang Prabang, had taken me to a small office space down the alley from his pagoda. It housed a not-for-profit organization, Big Brother Mouse, the NGO that my elderly female companion had pointed out on our cab ride into town from the airport. You could drop by every day/any day to practice English with young people or adults who wanted to improve their speaking and writing skills. Or you could sign up to take a van to the countryside, pay for your lunch, and spend the day in a village doing the same thing with students in a special pre-K-12 school—a perfect way to celebrate turning seventy-six, I decided.

The day's activities at the village school were anything but easy. There was a rigorous curriculum to cover, many times over, with small groups of eager elementary-aged kids who were dressed in slightly ragged, dusty uniforms. The smart boards currently used in U.S. schools were nonexistent. Instead, there were large posters with various images of animals and birds that the children could use to prompt sentences, statements, adjectives, and adverbs. I stood before them pointing to a picture and, depending on the task assigned, encouraged their participation. For their part, when they finished the lesson, they wanted to know why I didn't have games on my iPad. At the end of each round of posters, the children would dance wildly to K-Pop, expending pent-up energy before moving on to their next lesson.

I needed a break from their boundless energy, which was impervious to temperatures in the mid-nineties so, after a lunch of sticky rice and dry, spicy pork and chicken eaten with my fingers, I met with the older kids. They were boys and girls who should have been in the twelfth grade or beginning college but, because of circumstance and poverty, came to the village school for extra-curricular learning. I led them in a discussion about the ethics of being a student. We talked about attendance, cheating, and doing their work. They followed the conversation (with the occasional help of a translator) and remained very engaged— perhaps a difference between them and typical teenagers.

There was little equipment and no computers; in their place board games, decks of cards and even pick-up sticks littered the floor. The kids sat in small groups and played games with a volunteer, if one was available, or a teacher. One young man joined us for a math game played with a deck of cards. Each player gets four cards and then has to manipulate them to achieve a single answer. I can't really describe the game because I couldn't follow it; you have to be able to think in numbers, and I'm a word person. But the young man who joined the group was a math whiz— solving the puzzle every time in a matter of seconds. MIT would have loved to have him as a student. All I could think was *that will never happen.* Those thoughts still haunt me. Why didn't I figure out how to make the connection, make it happen. I had done it many times before. I fault the heat for dulling my brain. Still, I often wish I could return, find this young man and rectify my omission. One day I will and hopefully it won't be too little too late.

Eventually, I gave up on the cards and sat down with Inoke, one of the women who works for Big Brother Mouse, managing the volunteers at the village school. She had been very precise in her directions and didn't brook any deviation from the poster curriculum. I had not liked her very much, feeling constrained by the pedagogy. But then, while chatting, I learned her story—a story of forced marriage, divorce, and abandonment. A village girl, she had lost her children to her former spouse and had to survive on her wits and tenacity. After a number of jobs, each time learning a new skill and moving up to a better position, she wound up at the NGO—a place she had initially sought out for help learning English. By then she had her sons back because her ex-husband's new wife didn't want them; but they returned to her with nothing, not even a pair of shoes. As she talked I was able to understand my experience earlier that day.

There was a boy in one of my groups who wore broken sandals and an old, frayed uniform that was brown with age. At first, he didn't participate; he was shy and a little hostile. His embarrassed mother, Inoke, who had been watching his behavior, told me that he was her youngest son. When I suggested that she step away from the group, the little seven-year-old tore up the lesson! His English was terrific—considerably better than his mother's.

We bonded over our shared experiences. Divorce is a universal story, and my admiration and affection began to bubble up and spill out my eyes. I reached into my pocket and pulled out a hundred-dollar bill that I had intended to donate to the NGO; instead, I put it in her hand and squeezed her fingers around it, saying "For your sons, not the NGO. For them, okay?" The bill disappeared, and a smile fixed itself firmly on her face. I got back on the van to return to Luang Prabang. She waved as it pulled out of the play yard, and I let out a sigh—not exactly the exhalation of a do-gooder, and certainly not the smug emission of a philanthropist, but the sigh of someone who knows that she has done very little and needs to do much more.

I was exhausted and decided that the remainder of my birthday would be spent having an early dinner, then going straight to bed. However, the desk clerk at the guest house had asked me to stop by when I arrived back from my outing. When I got to the office, the entire staff was there—the Chinese manager, Ying Xia Shang, as well as two guests and the monk, Phra Bounthong. He had slipped out of the monastery and walked over to share in a surprise birthday celebration. At the hotel manager's request, the staff had bought a round chocolate layer cake from the French bakery in town. Across the top, written in white icing, was "H B Madame Garrison." Delight sparred with fatigue, but I managed to exchange pleasantries with everyone. There was a round of "Happy Birthday" in English, photos, and lots of smiles from me until my cheeks cramped.

The monk left without eating any cake. Monks are not allowed to eat after the noon meal. They are also not allowed out of the monastery at night, so Phra Bounthong had to sneak back in quickly before he was missed. I'm not sure if he had ever been to a birthday party with Western cake and singing. The other hotel guests left for an actual dinner, while I had a second piece of cake and called it dinner. The hotel manager told me that she had organized the party at the request of the staff, who didn't want me to celebrate my birthday alone. So there we were, a collection of strangers sharing a moment together . . . and a slice of cake. ■

CHAPTER PHOTO CREDIT: Hard to believe I made it to the bottom of the hole in the jungle cliff. *The Carole J. Garrison Family Archive.*

With the beautiful dancers on the Mekong River cruise. *The Carole J. Garrison Family Archive.*

On a break from learning English at the Brother Mouse village school. *The Carole J. Garrison Family Archive.*

The day I met the little monk preparing for a Boun Khao Pansa festival. *The Carole J. Garrison Family Archive.*

The Brother Mouse office in Luang Prabang. *The Carole J. Garrison Family Archive.*

Discovering the elephants and their mahouts on my jungle trek. *The Carole J. Garrison Family Archive.*

The village girls. *The Carole J. Garrison Family Archive.*

Trying to get my "good luck" bird to fly. *The Carole J. Garrison Family Archive.*

15 Fiji

I left Cambodia via a short layover in Singapore ready for my next destination. Even before I boarded the plane for the ten-hour flight from Singapore, I had the distinct impression that Fiji was going to be strange. The ground crew wouldn't let me enter the jet bridge until I showed proof of an outgoing flight. Besides not being very friendly, their behavior was quite odd, although the Fiji airport in Nadi was really nice. Modern, clean, and busy. There was even a native band to greet us passengers—large, dark-skinned men wearing bright floral shirts and dark blue cotton skirts, playing guitars and banjos.

I couldn't find a cab. Everyone was going to Suva, the capital, to try to catch a glimpse of Prince Harry and his American bride, Meghan, who were touring Australia and the South Pacific Islands; they would be in Suva the following day. Eventually I found a tourist office next to the currency exchange. After I booked a day tour, the smiling, sarong-clad woman hailed me a cab.

I wasn't prepared for the squalor of Nadi, a city on Fiji's main island. It didn't look like the Fiji I had seen on HGTV. The buildings were dilapidated; the cars were old; and the storefronts were a combination of Indian and inner-city general stores. My hotel, the JFK, was a rundown building on a small side road called Vunavou Street. The rooms were located above a small South Indian restaurant in the front and a nightclub in the back. I was greeted by two Fijian women, Betty and Milly, who smiled and reassured me that I would be just fine. "Quiet and clean," they said as they led me up to my eight-foot-square charmless, cheerless, cramped room with a large covered window facing the street. It bore no resemblance to the photo on Booking.com.

I threw my suitcase on the bed and went out to stretch my legs and decide whether I could actually stay there. I walked down the main street, observing school boys in long shorts or sarongs and girls in white or blue shifts, depending on the school they attended. Many of the men were huge and very dark, some heart-stopping handsome—a big mix of Fijian (descendants of Tanzanian Africans by way of Indonesia), East Indian, European and Australian. Men wore sarongs; women strolled in bright floral dresses or Indian saris.

The sign above the door said "Authentic Fiji Crafts." The windows were full of beautiful wood carvings, inlaid turtles, and large bowls. I was greeted by two men who, with total disregard for my jet lag, convinced me to imbibe a cup of Kava, Fiji's national and ceremonial welcoming drink. Of course, it came with a sales pitch, and now I own a lovely carved turtle!

Ear plugs and determination got me through the first night. I had scheduled a few tours with a *very local* tour agency. (The staff operated out of a hair salon and assured me that all proceeds stayed in the local community.) I decided not to move to new accommodations quite yet. I liked Betty and Milly, who made little animals out of towels like you find on cruise ships, and there were no bugs—although I would have to find a better place for breakfast.

On my first tour, I learned that Tom Cruise owns one of the 320 islands that make up Fiji. His is the only island inhabited with deer, which he imported from the United States. The late Raymond Burr, an orchid enthusiast, also lived in Fiji. The tour group, consisting of me and an Australian couple, visited the Sleeping Giant Garden—a large, lush botanical garden where Burr grew his orchids and plants. Our guide drove us to a nearby, typical Fijian village and pointed out the chief's house. It was easy to spot, because a chief's house is always in the village center and has the tallest roof. The homes of families belonging to the warrior tribe surrounded the chief's home. All the houses were modest and, in many cases, even primitive. Each village has a church, unless it happens to be a Hindu or Muslim village. The absence of a church is one way to determine whose village it is, but there is also a more colorful indication. Muslims paint their homes, schools, and buses green; Hindus put red flags on their homes. The guide told us how the first Christian missionary was eaten by locals, but assured us that Fijians are no longer cannibals. (I heard the same story from another traveler before I left Laos. However, Milly, at the hotel, said there were still some practicing cannibals in remote villages.) Our tour ended at the flamingo-pink Sri Siva Subramaniya Hindu temple that guards the southern entrance to Nadi—an outlandish reminder of the growing Hindu population of Fiji.

I followed the tour with a back massage, a nap, and a few minutes on the hotel's computer to try to connect with my online class that had started while I was in Laos. *Amazing that, despite the lack of dependable Wi-Fi and limited access to computers, I could still teach while tramping around the world. Teaching fed my brain; traveling fed my soul.* Then I went to the Port Denarau Marina. It was there that I made the decision to stay with Milly and Betty at the JFK. The marina could have been in Naples or Sanibel Island, Florida, down to some of the same franchises like the Hard Rock Café and the Bone Fish Grill. Although I wound up eating dinner with a pleasant enough family from New Zealand, I wanted nothing more than to return to Nadi, put my ear plugs in, and try to stay awake until 9:00 p.m. so that I could sleep through the music and the night.

On my next tour I visited the coral coast, where I walked along the surf, chatted with hunky fisherman, drank fresh coconut juice, and rejected the souvenir sellers who accepted "no" replies with smiles and kind words. This time I was joined by a mother and daughter from New Zealand. While I continued walking, the mom had her hair braided into cornrows and the daughter had an hour-long massage on the beach.

Our driver, a middle-aged Indian fellow, had a terrible sinus problem and breathed so loudly that I had to sit in the backseat just to be able to think. We left the beach, with its competing views of the surf and the magnificent Hilton resort, and drove to a lovely Fijian village where, after passing on the Kava ritual, we took a challenging hike up to a nearby waterfall. I wasn't prepared for the hike nor the cold freshwater streams that we had to cross to get there. Sometimes being the old lady comes in handy; the village women—our tour guides—were happy to hold my arm or wait while I caught my breath.

To my tummy's dismay, our driver took us to a typical Indian restaurant for lunch—whether it was owned by a relative or just his lunch preference, I wasn't sure. Fiji is a unique fusion of South India and Fiji island culture, which is simultaneously colorful and confusing. Restaurant food tends to be Indian, hot and spicy. Fijian food, mostly vegetables, is slow-cooked in the ground so that you have to be in a village to enjoy it. In addition to this culinary competition, politics is becoming more strained between the two ethnicities as they each vie for power and influence. The British brought Indians to the islands as cheap labor in the late 1920s, and they stayed. Now they account for a large percentage of the population and, thus, the political rivalry is heating up the airwaves. I got a good dose of the rhetoric while being driven around the island with car radios tuned to local talk shows.

The climate of Fiji is much like Hawaii's—perfect— and the surf and beaches are pristine. But my tour unmasked the poverty that exists alongside outrageous displays of wealth. Much of the coastal land and big resorts are on property leased or sold by Fijians, who remain in villages and the outlying islands. It's hard to tell whether the wealth is all foreign in origin or belongs to these unseen, ancient Fijian families. Sugar cane and tourism are the biggest revenue streams, and the locals welcome anyone who comes to pump money into the economy.

I think the phrase "saving the best for last" is actually a lyric from a popular song. For me, however, it describes my final tour—the one I had booked at the airport on arrival—and it was wonderful. My four companions on this tour were two young Chinese men from Hong Kong and an older, retired Australian couple. I suppose it was wonderful because it included a visit to a village school.

"*Bula!*" As soon as we walked into the school, we were greeted with shouts of "hello." I'm sure we were just a few in the procession of tourists who came to visit, and yet we were treated as special guests. After introducing ourselves, we were entertained, classroom by classroom, with songs and smiles. Like those in Laos, this school had no working computers—no technology at all, for that matter. But the blackboards and walls were covered with grade-appropriate materials for science, math, and spelling; posters reminded the students of the rules of good behavior. Children did not wear uniforms like in the town schools; most did wear shoes, however. All of them were eager to tell us about rugby.

From the school we went to a neighboring village for the best meal I had eaten in days. The *turanga ni koro* (village headman) greeted us and provided each of the women with a *sulu* (Fijian sarong) to tie around her waist. Once we were properly attired, the headman—in this case, the top security person in the village and a member of the warrior clan—invited us into his kitchen to help finish cooking our lunch. It was a vegetarian meal, cooked underground and then suffused with fresh-squeezed coconut juice. I wanted to stay there forever! Chengdu could keep its pandas; I wanted traditional Fijian food.

Eating requires yet another ceremony. Shoeless, we entered the large central room, sat cross-legged on the floor and, bowing our heads slightly, introduced ourselves. Before eating, guests are always invited to participate in a *yaqona*, a Kava-drinking ceremony. I wondered how many times a day our host had to drink this potent beverage, along with his guests. Eventually, we were permitted to dig in, using our hands and eating family-style.

Little children, who were not in school, danced and sang. Two villagers joined us and played guitars. The elderly Australian woman got up and danced, and the headman seemed bent on hugging me. A good, strong embrace by a big handsome Fijian man was okay with me.

Only one experience will remain in my memory longer than this remarkable day—my visit with Milly to her large village, which lies just outside the northern end of Nadi. It was my last day in Fiji. Milly had asked me the previous day if I would like to visit her home, her children, and her village. She seemed genuinely pleased when I accepted her invitation, and she was surprised when I returned from the tour and asked if she would still take me home with her. "Yes," she said. "We will walk to my village and take a cab back, if that's okay. I have to work at the nightclub tonight, and I need to change."

Nadi town, as the locals called it, was not much more than a few miles long, so I figured I could walk the distance. We set out at a quick pace and, thirty minutes later, arrived at a village of makeshift dwellings and cardboard bridges spanning puddles. Barefoot children, from babies to eight-year-olds, were playing here and there with runny noses. Milly, after introducing me to her three kids, a couple of cousins, and an aunt, abandoned me to get ready—"dolled-up," as her aunty called it—for her evening job.

One little girl playing amongst the gang of youngsters, a mulatto, was the product of a white great grandmother and her Fijian lover. If anyone took offense at her blue-green eyes and light, creamy skin, they didn't show it. I chatted with the women, watched the children play and chase chickens and pigs, and marveled at the relaxed attitude they seemed to take toward their living situation. I had just finished a glass of homemade lemonade when Milly reappeared, dressed in heels and a slinky dress, perfumed and made-up. She looked more like a woman on the hunt than a waitress at a club. We said our goodbyes; she kissed her kids; and we headed out to the main road. We walked a few blocks till we were able to hail a cab back into town. The cab driver stopped several blocks short of our destination and told us to get out because he had a fare to pick up. Aghast, I said that he was to take us to the JFK or I was not paying him. "Fine, don't pay me. Just go." Milly and I wasted no time tumbling out of the cab. She looked at me with new-found admiration.

I left Milly and Betty the last of my Opium perfume along with some makeup, a pair of sandals, and a few blouses that I didn't want to drag home. I'm not sure I could have managed another night at the JFK, but I was glad that I had stayed there and not moved out of town. By the end of my few days in Nadi, the locals knew me, waved to me as I sat at a local coffee shop in the early morning, told their children to say "bula," and smiled when we passed on the street.

It was time to end this journey. Time to go home, vote for any reasonable candidates I could find on the ballot, and hope we could turn the tide against race-baiters, misogynists, anti-intellectuals, and climate change deniers. Guess I still believe that every vote counts. Mass emails to the friends back home who followed my journey would end, and I would start to send new ones to the wonderful friends I'd made along the way, or to old friends who had given me shelter and love throughout this journey.

Next stop: Los Angeles, and then home to West Virginia. ■

CHAPTER PHOTO CREDIT: Drinking kava, the country's national drink. *The Carole J. Garrison Family Archive.*

The wealthy port-side of Fiji. *The Carole J. Garrison Family Archive.*

Enjoying a taste of Navala village life. *The Carole J. Garrison Family Archive.*

Enthusiasm at the Navala village school. *The Carole J. Garrison Family Archive.*

Watching the children walk to school in Nadi town. *The Carole J. Garrison Family Archive.*

Treking out to the waterfall. *The Carole J. Garrison Family Archive.*

The children of Milly's village. *The Carole J. Garrison Family Archive.*

Sharing a traditional lunch at Navala village. *The Carole J. Garrison Family Archive.*

Making friends on the Fiji beach. *The Carole J. Garrison Family Archive.*

Taking in the Fiji countryside. *The Carole J. Garrison Family Archive.*

EPILOGUE

Mixed in with the mountain of junk mail, a few birthday cards, and several Amazon packages containing things I had ordered (like my favorite hair gel, so the stuff would be there when I got home) was a large UPS box postmarked Nepal. Christmas came early and I must admit relieved that I had shopped. It took considerably longer to catch up with my colleague than to open mail, Victor—close to three months. The weather, the flu, and winter holidays all combined to make driving down to visit him in Kentucky a series of no-gos. Our reunion was sweet, but his recuperation was slow, and it was obvious that Victor still had a way to go before he fully recovered. His wife, Jana, and I commiserated about how frail he looked, and we cut brunch short because Victor needed a nap. Actually, I did, too. We hugged and Jana whispered, "Keep turning those prayer wheels."

In each country I had used an app to send postcards to the fourth graders at the inner-city elementary school where I read to them weekly. When I returned, the kids added up the distance I had traveled from point to point—a total of 27,000 miles. One little boy raised his hand, apprehension darkening his face. "Yes?" I asked. "Dr. G., do your feet hurt?" I thanked him for his concern and, trying not to laugh, reminded him that they were air miles, not hiking miles.

When I was a young mother living in Miami, Florida, I would pack my toddler daughter into her car seat, grab a couple of PB&J sandwiches and a thermos of milk, and head for the airport's perimeter road. There I would park, turn the car radio to the control tower frequency, and listen as we watched the planes take off and land. It was one of my favorite activities. At that time, these excursions were about the only kind of travel I could afford. Oh, there was the occasional family outing to one of Florida's famous tourist attractions, but I found them too plastic, too phony. Except for Cape Canaveral. Back then, I wanted to be on one of those planes taking off from Miami International Airport—or, better yet, at the Cape, strapped into a rocket ship to the moon.

It wasn't until midlife that I had the opportunity to travel, and travel I have—by car, rail, plane, ship, and on foot. If someone asked me whether I wanted to go somewhere that I had never been, there was only one answer: yes. When yes was my response to an invitation by a friend to visit her home in Isfahan, Iran, at the height of the Iraq War (amid some widely televised beheadings), my children had panic attacks. On another occasion, I went to Mexico with an artist friend. We took only pastels, no cameras. Since we had no itinerary, we just crisscrossed the country from place to place as transportation became available or the spirit moved us. One night, after arriving too late in a town to find a place to stay, we convinced a young man to take us to his *tia's* house. She and her three small *niñas* were away, so we slept in tiny beds with tiny pillows. Sometime during the night, the young man panicked and begged us to leave. I think he thought we were hatchet murderers. We managed to convince him to let us stay until dawn.

By the time I took my first trip around the world in the late 1980s with my mother, I had done some academic traveling—mainly to destinations in the United States and Canada. I began crossing states and major cities off my wall map, along with some Western European countries. On the round-the-world trip, my mom and I traveled for several months, staying mostly with former physics students who had studied with my then-husband. As the professor's wife, with the additional advantage of traveling with an elderly mother, I was hosted and entertained in China, Hong Kong, India, and Thailand. That was the trip where I left her in New Delhi and went alone to Nepal. Mom and I were compatible travelers, except that she had a strict rule about not going out at night. We didn't then. Now I don't, either.

Another time, my elder brother invited me along to be my mother's roommate on a trip to South Africa and Rhodesia when she wanted to go on safari for her eighty-fifth birthday. On that occasion, I had a bit of a tiff with my sister-in-law because I wouldn't pull my mother's carry-on bag. Mom and I had long ago made a pledge never to pack more than we could carry ourselves. Marlene was so put out with me that she thrust my brother's photography equipment into my arms and ordered, "Carry this!" Since they were footing the bill, I carried my brother's camera equipment; mom took care of her own stuff. Consulting with the military on women's issues provided a free opportunity to travel, courtesy of the Department of Defense, as did volunteering for UNTAC, the United Nations peacekeeping mission in Cambodia. I traveled to military bases the world over and, after UNTAC, I set out to visit the distant friends I'd made while supervising the Cambodian election.

I never gave wandering much thought. You travel somewhere; you marvel at the sights; you inhale the smells and taste the flavors of your surroundings. You make friends of strangers and renew ties to old friends. I am not a careful traveler. I don't have specific agendas for must-see places, and I don't spend a lot of time reflecting on what I have seen. I read less than fifteen percent of the little placards in museums, rarely sit for long in front of any masterpiece, or prepare myself for an exhibit. Shamefully, I've been known not to get past a museum gift shop, without seeing any galleries whatsoever. But I do know this with certainty. I will continue to be a wanderer . . . until I can't. ∎

CHAPTER PHOTO CREDIT: The end of my journey. *The Carole J. Garrison Family Archive.*

ABOUT THE AUTHOR

PHOTO CREDIT: Missica Skeens/Missica Photography

CAROLE J. GARRISON is a former police officer, retired professor, activist and passionate humanitarian. After a stint as a suburban housewife and mother in Miami, she joined the Atlanta Bureau of Police Services in the early 1970s as one of a handful of women police officers but shifted to education after receiving her PhD from Ohio State University. During her career as an educator, she helped launch the University of Akron's Women's Studies program, was inducted into the Ohio Women's Hall of Fame, was vice president of Ohio's first women's commission, appointed by the U.S. president to the Department of Defense Committee on the Status of Women in the Military, and volunteered with the UN to help supervise Cambodia's first democratic election. In 1993, she returned to Akron to teach, but thee years later she returned to Cambodia and served as executive director of the Cooperation Committee for Cambodia, a network of humanitarian and developmental non-governmental organizations (NGO).

Her work has appeared in *VietNow Nation Magazine, The Sacrifice: What Would You Give? An Anthology of Inspirational Essays* (2014), *WHAT DOES IT MEAN TO BE WHITE IN AMERICA? Breaking the White Code of Silence, A Collection of Personal Narratives* (2016), and placed in the WOW! Women On Writing, Winter 2016 Flash Fiction contest, *The Wait.* She published her first book, *The Fourth Moment: Journeys from the Known to the Unknown, A Memoir* in 2017.

Today, Garrison resides in Ona, West Virginia. Although retired as chair of the Department of Criminal Justice and Police Studies at Eastern Kentucky University, she continues to teach applied ethics and policing courses online. When not teaching or writing, she serves as an executive board member of the Friends of WV Public Broadcasting, Chair of the Board of Unlimited Future, a local Huntington business incubator, a docent at the Huntington Museum of Art, and is a member of the Huntington Women's Leadership Caucus. She is also a reader for fourth grade at Altizer Elementary School and a Girls on The Run volunteer at Nichols Elementary School. www.cjgarrison.com. ∎

OTHER BOOKS BY 2LEAF PRESS

2LEAF PRESS challenges the status quo by publishing alternative fiction, non-fiction, poetry and bilingual works by activists, academics, poets and authors dedicated to diversity and social justice with scholarship that is accessible to the general public. 2LEAF PRESS produces high quality and beautifully produced hardcover, paperback and ebook formats through our series: *2LP Explorations in Diversity*, *2LP University Books*, *2LP Classics*, *2LP Translations*, *Nuyorican World Series*, and *2LP Current Affairs, Culture & Politics*. Below is a selection of 2LEAF PRESS' published titles.

2LP EXPLORATIONS IN DIVERSITY

Substance of Fire: Gender and Race in the College Classroom
by Claire Millikin
Foreword by R. Joseph Rodríguez,
Afterword by Richard Delgado
Contributors Riley Blanks, Blake Calhoun, Rox Trujillo

Black Lives Have Always Mattered
A Collection of Essays, Poems, and Personal Narratives
Edited by Abiodun Oyewole

The Beiging of America:
Personal Narratives about Being Mixed Race in the 21st Century
Edited by Cathy J. Schlund-Vials, Sean Frederick Forbes,
Tara Betts, with an Afterword by Heidi Durrow

What Does it Mean to be White in America?
Breaking the White Code of Silence, A Collection of Personal Narratives
Edited by Gabrielle David and Sean Frederick Forbes

Introduction by Debby Irving and Afterword by Tara Betts

2LP CLASSICS
Adventures in Black and White
Edited and with a critical introduction by Tara Betts
by Philippa Duke Schuyler

Monsters: Mary Shelley's Frankenstein and Mathilda
by Mary Shelley, edited by Claire Millikin Raymond

2LP TRANSLATIONS
Birds on the Kiswar Tree
by Odi Gonzales, Translated by Lynn Levin
Bilingual: English/Spanish

Incessant Beauty, A Bilingual Anthology
by Ana Rossetti, Edited and Translated by Carmela Ferradáns
Bilingual: English/Spanish

NUYORICAN WORLD SERIES
Our Nuyorican Thing, The Birth of a Self-Made Identity
by Samuel Carrion Diaz, with an Introduction by Urayoán
Noel
Bilingual: English/Spanish

Hey Yo! Yo Soy!, 40 Years of Nuyorican Street Poetry,
The Collected Works of Jesús Papoleto Meléndez
Bilingual: English/Spanish

LITERARY NONFICTION
No Vacancy; Homeless Women in Paradise
by Michael Reid

The Beauty of Being, A Collection of Fables, Short Stories & Essays
by Abiodun Oyewole

WHEREABOUTS: Stepping Out of Place,

An Outside in Literary & Travel Magazine Anthology
Edited by Brandi Dawn Henderson

PLAYS
Rivers of Women, The Play
by Shirley Bradley LeFlore
with photographs by Michael J. Bracey

AUTOBIOGRAPHIES/MEMOIRS/BIOGRAPHIES
Trailblazers, Black Women Who Helped Make America Great
American Firsts/American Icons
by Gabrielle David

Mother of Orphans
The True and Curious Story of Irish Alice, A Colored Man's Widow
by Dedria Humphries Barker

Strength of Soul
by Naomi Raquel Enright

Dream of the Water Children:
Memory and Mourning in the Black Pacific
by Fredrick D. Kakinami Cloyd
Foreword by Velina Hasu Houston
Introduction by Gerald Horne
Edited by Karen Chau

The Fourth Moment: Journeys from the Known to the Unknown, A
Memoir
by Carole J. Garrison, Introduction by Sarah Willis

POETRY
PAPOLÍTICO, Poems of a Political Persuasion
by Jesús Papoleto Meléndez
with an Introduction by Joel Kovel and DeeDee Halleck

Critics of Mystery Marvel, Collected Poems
by Youssef Alaoui, with an Introduction by Laila Halaby

shrimp
by jason vasser-elong, with an Introduction by Michael Castro

The Revlon Slough, New and Selected Poems
by Ray DiZazzo, with an Introduction by Claire Millikin

Written Eye: Visuals/Verse
by A. Robert Lee

A Country Without Borders: Poems and Stories of Kashmir
by Lalita Pandit Hogan, with an Introduction by Frederick Luis
Aldama

Branches of the Tree of Life
The Collected Poems of Abiodun Oyewole 1969-2013
by Abiodun Oyewole, edited by Gabrielle David
with an Introduction by Betty J. Dopson

2Leaf Press is owned and operated by 2Leaf Press Inc. a Florida-based nonprofit organization that publishes and promotes multi-cultural literature.

FLORIDA | NEW YORK
www.2leafpress.org